BEARING FRUIT

in God's Family

This book belongs to: ____________________

BEARING FRUIT
in God's Family

A COURSE IN PERSONAL DISCIPLESHIP TO STRENGTHEN YOUR WALK WITH GOD

THE 2:7 SERIES

3

NAVPRESS

A NavPress resource published in alliance with Tyndale House Publishers, Inc.

NCM

NAVIGATOR **CHURCH** MINISTRIES

NAVPRESS®

NavPress is the publishing ministry of The Navigators, an international Christian organization and leader in personal spiritual development. NavPress is committed to helping people grow spiritually and enjoy lives of meaning and hope through personal and group resources that are biblically rooted, culturally relevant, and highly practical.

For more information, visit www.NavPress.com.

Bearing Fruit in God's Family: A Course in Personal Discipleship to Strengthen Your Walk with God

A NavPress resource published in alliance with Tyndale House Publishers, Inc.

For information about special discounts for bulk purchases, please contact Tyndale House Publishers at csresponse@tyndale.com, or call 1-800-323-9400.

ISBN 978-1-61521-637-6

Printed in the United States of America

23 22 21 20 19 18 17
13 12 11 10 9 8 7

ACKNOWLEDGMENT

We are grateful for the dedicated efforts of Ron Oertli, who originated the concept of The 2:7 Series and is its principal author. Ron is also the key person responsible for this updated edition. This discipleship training approach began in Denver in 1970 and continues to be highly effective in many places around the world.

CONTENTS

MY COMPLETION RECORD

As you complete each item, ask someone in your group to sign off for that item with his or her initials and the calendar date.

SCRIPTURE MEMORY	INITIALS	DATE
Required verses: "Proclaim Christ"		
"All Have Sinned"—Romans 3:23		
"Sin's Penalty"—Romans 6:23		
"Christ Paid the Penalty"—Romans 5:8		
"Salvation Not by Works"—Ephesians 2:8-9		
"Must Receive Christ"—John 1:12		
"Assurance of Salvation"—1 John 5:13		
Recommended but optional verses: "Proclaim Christ"		
"All Have Sinned"—Isaiah 53:6		
"Sin's Penalty"—Hebrews 9:27		
"Christ Paid the Penalty"—1 Peter 3:18		
"Salvation Not by Works"—Titus 3:5		
"Must Receive Christ"—Romans 10:9-10		
"Assurance of Salvation"—John 5:24		
Quoted the 6 required "Proclaim Christ" verses		
Quoted all 12 "Proclaim Christ" verses		
Quoted your "Live the New Life" verses from book 2		
Reviewed your "Live the New Life" verses for 14 consecutive days		
QUIET TIME		
Completed *My Reading Highlights* for 14 consecutive days		
WITNESS		
Identified with Christ in a relating activity (pages 18–19)		
Told "My Story" with or without notes in less than 4 minutes		
Used Evangelism Prayer List for 7 consecutive days		
Gave The Bridge Illustration:		
Outline		
"Lecture Presentation 1"		
"Lecture Presentation 2"		
BIBLE STUDY		
Session 3—The Call to Fruitful Living (pages 28–35)		
Session 5—Love in Action (pages 44–49)		
Session 6—Purity of Life (pages 52–58)		
Session 8—Integrity in Living (pages 71–75)		
Session 11—Character in Action (pages 91–97)		

OTHER		
Completed "Ways to Meditate on Scripture: Part 1" (pages 14–18)		
Completed "Ways to Meditate on Scripture: Part 2" (pages 22–24)		
Completed "Verse Analysis of Matthew 6:33" (pages 77–80)		
Completed "Priorities: Part 1" (pages 80–84)		
Studied "Priorities: Part 2" (pages 85–90)		
LEADER'S CHECK		
Graduated from *Bearing Fruit in God's Family* (book 3)		

ABBREVIATIONS FOR BIBLE VERSIONS

Unless otherwise identified, Scripture quotations are from the *Holy Bible: New International Version*. You can refer to this list when you encounter unfamiliar Bible version abbreviations.

- (AMP) The Amplified Bible
- (ESV) English Standard Version
- (KJV) King James Version
- (MLB) Modern Language Bible: The Berkeley Version in Modern English
- (MSG) The Message
- (NASB) New American Standard Bible
- (NCV) New Century Version
- (NIV) New International Version
- (NKJV) New King James Version
- (NLT) New Living Translation
- (NRSV) New Revised Standard Version
- (PH) The New Testament in Modern English (J. B. Phillips)

SESSION 1

OUTLINE OF THIS SESSION

1. Open the session in prayer.
2. Go over "Reviewing the Goals of Book 2 in The 2:7 Series" (pages 9–10).
3. Preview book 3 by looking over *My Completion Record* (pages 7–8).
4. Survey "Scripture Memory Guide—Week 1" (pages 10–11).
5. Read "The *TMS* in Book 3" (pages 11–13).
6. Complete "Ways to Meditate on Scripture: Part 1" (pages 14–18).
   a. Write out a paraphrase of 2 Timothy 3:16.
   b. Ask yourself questions on Hebrews 10:24-25.
7. Discuss current use of the evangelism prayer list.
8. Read and discuss "Openly Identifying with Christ" (pages 18–19).
9. Read "Assignment for Session 2" (page 20).
10. Close the session in prayer.

REVIEWING THE GOALS OF BOOK 2 IN THE 2:7 SERIES

The goals of book 2 were:

1. To experience a more consistent and meaningful quiet time by:
   a. Combining meaningful Bible reading and prayer
   b. Succeeding in having fourteen consecutive quiet times during the course
   c. Recording daily quiet-time thoughts and how they impressed you on *My Reading Highlights*
   d. Growing in your ability to share key quiet-time thoughts with others in the group
2. To quote accurately the five or six Scripture memory verses you learned in book 1
3. To memorize at least six *TMS* verses from "Live the New Life," which correlate with The Wheel Illustration
4. To study and discuss *My Heart—Christ's Home*, by Robert Boyd Munger
5. To experience an Extended Time with God after reading and discussing material on the subject
6. To complete five Bible studies and discuss each of them in your 2:7 group

7. To tell your "My Story" in less than four minutes using only an outline on an index card
8. To relate to a non-Christian friend through a nonspiritual activity

SCRIPTURE MEMORY GUIDE—WEEK 1

EXCERPTS FROM THE *TOPICAL MEMORY SYSTEM (TMS)*

You're Under Way

Book 2 got you off to a good start with your completion of valuable verses on "Live the New Life" from the *Topical Memory System*. You have begun to enjoy some of the benefits that Scripture memory can bring. Now you want to keep up your momentum as you tackle verses on "Proclaim Christ," wonderful verses you can use as you share your faith.

During this course, you will again have helpful memory suggestions each week in the Scripture memory guides. The segments "About the Verses" and "Your Weekly Plan" will contribute to your success.

What to Expect

Scripture memory is personally enriching and helps in at least three major areas: having victory over temptation, overcoming anxiety, and witnessing effectively. In book 3, you will learn verses that can greatly contribute to your effectiveness in witnessing.

Memorize and Review from Verse Cards

During this course, you'll continue to either download and print your verse cards or put your memory verses on a blank business card or index card. Write them out or use your printer. On the front of the card, put the topic, reference, verse, and reference.

Use the Buddy System

Proverbs 27:17 says that "as iron sharpens iron, a friend sharpens a friend" (NLT). There's a parallel thought in Ecclesiates 4:9-10: "Two people can accomplish more than twice as much as one. . . . If one person falls, the other can reach out and help" (NLT). We all need encouragement in our Christian lives, and this surely applies to memorizing Scripture.

Ask someone else in your 2:7 group to get together with you outside of class to review each other's verses. You may also want to talk over any difficulties you are having, but, above all, share how God is using the verses in your lives. This will help both of you succeed in Scripture memory.

Knowledge and Application

Some Christians confuse Bible knowledge with spiritual maturity, assuming that knowing more about the Bible automatically makes a person a better Christian. This is not necessarily true. The Pharisees knew the

Old Testament, yet they were spiritually blind. The key to spiritual maturity is sincere and consistent application of God's Word to life.

The apostle Paul addressed the Corinthian believers as fleshly, unspiritual babes in Christ. He had to feed them milk instead of solid spiritual food. They took pride in wisdom and logic and may have understood the deeper truths Paul wanted to impart to them. But their lives contradicted what they professed to believe. Jealousy and strife split their ranks, and they behaved like ordinary, unregenerate people. Their lives were too much like those of the unbelievers in Corinth. What an indictment! They needed to apply the Word of God to their daily living.

Picture the Verse

We remember pictures more easily than words or concepts. If you find it difficult to connect a particular verse with its topic and reference, try forming a mental picture of the verse based on its content, context, or some other feature that will help you remember. The picture can become the mental hook you use later to draw the verse from your memory. It helps if you make the image as unusual or striking as possible.

For example, consider two verses in book 2 on witnessing: Matthew 4:19 and Romans 1:16. Associate the first verse with Christ and the second with Paul. Picture Jesus standing on a beach by the Sea of Galilee. Two fishermen are tending their nets when He calls out, "Come, follow me, and I will make you fishers of men." Fix this scene in your mind. Associate the picture with the topic of witnessing and with the reference Matthew 4:19.

Paul didn't write the book of Romans from Rome, but because it was addressed to the believers there, you might picture Paul standing in the Roman Forum or Colosseum speaking out to the pagan citizens, "I am not ashamed of the gospel because it is the power of God for the salvation of everyone who believes: first for the Jew, then for the Gentile." Associate this picture with the topic of witnessing and with the reference Romans 1:16.

You won't create a picture for every verse, but it is helpful for verses that you find difficult to remember by ordinary means.

THE *TMS* IN BOOK 3

You may recall that the whole *Topical Memory System* contains sixty memory verses. Each topic (A through E) has six subtopics. You can find more information about the *TMS* and other Scripture memory helps at www.2-7series.org.

A. Live the New Life	12 verses
B. Proclaim Christ	12 verses
C. Rely on God's Resources	12 verses
D. Be Christ's Disciple	12 verses
E. Grow in Christlikeness	12 verses

In book 2, you memorized verses from "Live the New Life." Here in book 3, you'll memorize verses from "Proclaim Christ." These are key verses you can use for explaining the gospel to others. You will use these memorized verses for the rest of your life; you want them at your fingertips, in the front of your mind.

So why not give yourself a gift? Go for memorizing all twelve verses while you are with friends in a positive Scripture memory environment. As you follow proven Scripture memory principles and guidelines, you will excel, but it will take consistent work. Memorized key verses become tools readily available for the Holy Spirit to use through you. Here are the "Proclaim Christ" verses:

Proclaim Christ (*TMS*)	**Required:**	**Recommended but Optional:**
All Have Sinned	Romans 3:23	Isaiah 53:6
Sin's Penalty	Romans 6:23	Hebrews 9:27
Christ Paid the Penalty	Romans 5:8	1 Peter 3:18
Salvation Not by Works	Ephesians 2:8-9	Titus 3:5
Must Receive Christ	John 1:12	Romans 10:9-10
Assurance of Salvation	1 John 5:13	John 5:24

Plan to end book 3 with the ability to skillfully quote all the verses you have memorized in The 2:7 Series. By the end of this course you will have memorized at least seventeen verses. That's great! You may even have memorized all twenty-nine verses. You may have memorized more than seventeen but less than twenty-nine. Whatever your life circumstances have allowed you to do, good work! You will have those verses readily available for recall to apply to your own life or to use in helping others. Plan to keep those verses sharp for a lifetime!

Your book 1 verses were:

Beginning with Christ	**Required:**	**Recommended but Optional:**
Assurance of Salvation	1 John 5:11-12	
Assurance of Answered Prayer	John 16:24	
Assurance of Victory	1 Corinthians 10:13	
Assurance of Forgiveness	1 John 1:9	

Beginning with Christ	**Required:**	**Recommended but Optional:**
Assurance of Guidance	Proverbs 3:5-6	
Optional Outreach Verse:		John 5:24

Your book 2 verses were:

Live the New Life (*TMS*)	**Required:**	**Recommended but Optional:**
Christ the Center	2 Corinthians 5:17	Galatians 2:20
Obedience to Christ	Romans 12:1	John 14:21
The Word	2 Timothy 3:16	Joshua 1:8
Prayer	John 15:7	Philippians 4:6-7
Fellowship	Hebrews 10:24-25	1 John 1:3
Witnessing	Matthew 4:19	Romans 1:16

MEDITATION: AN AID TO APPLICATION

One of the most beneficial reasons for memorizing Scripture verses is that it stimulates us to meditate on their content. During this course, you will be doing an exercise (pages 14–18) to increase your ability to meditate on passages of Scripture.

A valuable part of your Scripture memory program is meditating on verses you have learned. Not only will this enable you to retain them in your memory with accuracy, but as you reflect on and consider their contents, you will experience challenges, encouragement, and motivation. Remember God's instruction to Joshua: "Do not let this Book of the Law depart from your mouth; meditate on it day and night, so that you may be careful to do everything written in it. Then you will be prosperous and successful" (Joshua 1:8).

IMPORTANCE OF DAILY REVIEW

Continual review is the key to having a grasp on the verses you already know. An excellent goal by the end of book 3 would be having the ability to comfortably and accurately quote all of your memory verses from books 1–3, along with the topic for each of those verses. Plan to not only complete your memory assignments each week in book 3 but also quote daily the topics and references of all the verses you have learned.

Scripture memory and meditation are strategic parts of the discipleship training in which you are involved. They promote your spiritual development and lay the foundation for future spiritual growth. You will agree then with the psalmist: "Oh, how I love your law! I meditate on it all day long" (Psalm 119:97).

WAYS TO MEDITATE ON SCRIPTURE: PART 1

A GROUP EXERCISE

Blessed is the man
who does not walk in the counsel of the wicked
or stand in the way of sinners
or sit in the seat of mockers.
But his delight is in the law of the Lord,
and on his law he meditates day and night.
He is like a tree planted by streams of water,
which yields its fruit in season
and whose leaf does not wither.
Whatever he does prospers. (Psalm 1:1-3)

WHAT IS MEDITATION?

Meditation is the act of reflecting on, pondering, musing over, or contemplating. Meditation is *not* mind-wandering or indulging in "mental drifting"; instead it has form and an object. Bible verses and scriptural concepts are the focus of a Christian's meditation.

When we meditate, we spend a few moments directing our thoughts to a single subject. Meditation is thinking with a purpose. Meditation is not a solemn, academic exercise. It requires an attitude of curiosity and expectation, leading to exciting discoveries, refreshment of spirit, and transformation of character. It brings reward and benefit. When we meditate, we purposefully sort through information for clarification, application, categorization, and assimilation.

FURTHER INSIGHT INTO MEDITATION

The Message expresses Joshua 1:8 in a wonderful way:

> And don't for a minute let this Book . . . be out of mind. Ponder and meditate on it day and night, making sure you practice everything written in it. Then you'll get where you're going; then you'll succeed.

Meditation helps move biblical truth into everyday living patterns through personal, practical application. During this class session, you'll have the opportunity to practice two methods of meditation (pages 15–18). As part of your homework for next week, you will practice four additional methods of meditation (pages 22–24) for a total of six methods.

1—Paraphrase

The first method of meditation your group will practice is writing a paraphrase. As you attempt to put a verse or passage into your own words, you come to understand it more clearly. Some exciting insights often result from writing a paraphrase.

On the lines on pages 15–16, write out 2 Timothy 3:16 in your own words, using the following translations and paraphrases to help you complete this part of your work. (You may want to use more words in your paraphrase than are in the original verse.)

VARIOUS TRANSLATIONS AND PARAPHRASES OF 2 TIMOTHY 3:16

> All Scripture is God-breathed and is useful for teaching, rebuking, correcting and training in righteousness. (NIV)

> All Scripture is given by inspiration of God, and is profitable for doctrine, for reproof, for correction, for instruction in righteousness. (NKJV)

> All Scripture is inspired by God and profitable for teaching, for reproof, for correction, for training in righteousness. (NASB)

> All Scripture is inspired by God and is useful to teach us what is true and to make us realize what is wrong in our lives. It straightens us out and teaches us to do what is right. (NLT)

> All Scripture is inspired by God and is useful for teaching, for reproof, for correction, and for training in righteousness. (NRSV)

> Every Scripture is God-breathed (given by His inspiration) and profitable for instruction, for reproof and conviction of sin, for correction of error and discipline in obedience, [and] for training in righteousness (in holy living, in conformity to God's will in thought, purpose, and action). (AMP)

MY PARAPHRASE OF 2 TIMOTHY 3:16

2—Questions

A second method of meditation is to ask questions about a verse or passage (What does it say? What does it mean?) Two methods for asking those questions are:

1. Asking *who, what, when, where, why,* and *how* questions
2. Jotting down random questions that come to mind as you reflect on the passage

Some of the questions you ask may have immediate answers; others may not. Asking the questions becomes a way to think through a passage.

On the lines on page 18, please jot down some of the questions and answers that come to mind as you meditate on Hebrews 10:24-25, using the translations and paraphrases that follow to help you. You might begin by asking *who, what, when, where, why,* and *how* questions.

VARIOUS TRANSLATIONS AND PARAPHRASES OF HEBREWS 10:24-25

Let us consider how we may spur one another on toward love and good deeds. Let us not give up meeting together, as some are in the habit of doing, but let us encourage one another—and all the more as you see the Day approaching. (NIV)

And let us consider one another in order to stir up love and good works, not forsaking the assembling of ourselves together, as is the manner of some, but exhorting one another, and so much the more as you see the Day approaching. (NKJV)

And let us consider how to stimulate one another to love and good deeds, not forsaking our own assembling together, as is the habit of some, but encouraging one another, and all the more, as you see the day drawing near. (NASB)

Think of ways to encourage one another to outbursts of love and good deeds. And let us not neglect our meeting together, as some people do, but encourage and warn each other, especially now that the day of his coming back again is drawing near. (NLT)

And let us consider how to provoke one another to love and good deeds, not neglecting to meet together, as is the habit of some, but encouraging one another, and all the more as you see the Day approaching. (NRSV)

And let us consider and give attentive, continuous care to watching over one another, studying how we may stir up (stimulate and incite) to love and helpful deeds and noble activities, not forsaking or neglecting to assemble together [as believers], as is the habit of some people, but admonishing (warning, urging, and encouraging) one another, and all the more faithfully as you see the day approaching. (AMP)

QUESTIONS ABOUT HEBREWS 10:24-25

MEDITATION EXERCISES IN SESSION 2

In session 1, you have used two techniques for meditating on Scripture: paraphrase and questions. In session 2, "How to Meditate on Scripture: Part 2," you will experience four more meditation approaches: prayer, emphasis, cross-reference, and application.

OPENLY IDENTIFYING WITH CHRIST

During book 2, you had an assignment to participate in at least one "non-spiritual" activity with a non-Christian. Since then, you have probably been in various activities with that individual and other people who have not yet come to faith in Christ. As you know, spending time together is the primary way to develop friendship and openness with another person.

One assignment here in book 3 is to openly identify with Christ when you are with a pre-Christian acquaintance. Some call this "flying the flag." Old sailing ships flew the flag of their country so they could be identified from a distance by another ship. They were "flying the flag" of the country for whom they held allegiance. There is a point when a Christian needs to verbally begin "flying the flag"—not in a pushy way, but naturally and openly.

To openly identify with Christ does not mean giving your complete testimony or sharing the gospel. It simply means making a statement or comment that identifies you with Christ. It is wise to prepare what you might like to say when you have the opportunity. You could refer to something you heard in a sermon at church or something your child heard in Sunday school. You could refer to something Christ said in one of the gospels. You could make a brief statement about praying for someone or something. Be direct enough to be understood. Be confident yet gentle. Avoid sounding defensive.

> The Lord's servants must not quarrel but must be kind to everyone. They must be able to teach effectively and be patient with difficult people. They should gently teach those who oppose the truth. Perhaps God will change those people's hearts, and they will believe the truth.
>
> —2 Timothy 2:24-25 (NLT)

It is good to identify with Christ early in a friendship. The longer you go in a friendship without identifying with Christ, the harder it becomes to share your faith with that person. Pray for wisdom and boldness, make a plan, and carry it out in a gracious manner.

You may remember the conversation between God and Jeremiah in Jeremiah 1:6-8. Jeremiah spoke first.

> "Ah, Sovereign Lord," I said, "I do not know how to speak; I am only a child."
>
> But the Lord said to me, "Do not say, 'I am only a child.' You must go to everyone I send you to and say whatever I command you. Do not be afraid of them, for I am with you and will rescue you," declares the Lord.

You, too, may sometimes feel fearful or uneasy, but God will give you the courage and wisdom to say what needs to be said. Later you can build on this brief spiritual conversation.

ASSIGNMENT FOR SESSION 2

1. Scripture Memory: Study and complete "Scripture Memory Guide—Week 2" (pages 21–22). Memorize the verse(s) on "All Have Sinned": Romans 3:23 and Isaiah 53:6 (recommended but optional).
2. Quiet Time: Continue reading, marking, responding back to God in prayer, recording on *My Reading Highlights*, and using a prayer sheet.
3. Evangelism: Perhaps you will be one of those to tell "My Story" in class with or without notes in less than four minutes.
4. Other: Complete "Ways to Meditate on Scripture: Part 2" (pages 22–24). Meditation should not be hurried; take your time and enjoy the exercises.

SESSION 2

OUTLINE OF THIS SESSION

1. Open the session in prayer.
2. Break into verse review groups and quote the verse(s) on "All Have Sinned": Romans 3:23 and Isaiah 53:6 (recommended but optional). Work at getting anything signed that you can on *My Completion Record*. If you are able to memorize more than the required verse(s), get sign-off on those as well.
3. Share some quiet-time thoughts from *My Reading Highlights*.
4. Discuss "Ways to Meditate on Scripture: Part 2" (pages 22–24).
5. Listen to two or three group members tell their "My Story" with or without notes in less than four minutes.
6. Read "Introduction to Bible Study—Book 3" (pages 24–25).
7. Read "Assignment for Session 3" (page 25).
8. Close the session in prayer.

SCRIPTURE MEMORY GUIDE—WEEK 2

Moving Forward

You have three things to work with each week as you study the new memory verses on the topics of *Proclaim Christ*:

1. **Your Memory Cards**—to use daily (all the *Proclaim Christ* verses are listed on page 12)
2. **About the Verses**—to make the verses more meaningful and easier to learn and apply
3. **Your Weekly Plan**—to help you progress step-by-step in your memory work and avoid pitfalls

About the Verses

***TMS*-SERIES B:**
PROCLAIM CHRIST

As witnesses for Jesus Christ, we have two things to share: *our story* of how we found Christ and what He means to us now, and *the gospel*, God's plan of salvation. The gospel explains the deep need of all people, God's love for every individual, and Christ's death on the cross to make eternal life possible.

The topics and verses in this series form a usable outline for presenting the gospel. These memory verses can help you become more skillful in proclaiming Christ.

TOPIC 1: ALL HAVE SINNED

Life in the twenty-first century presents seemingly insurmountable problems of war, crime, racial strife, and violence of all kinds. Experts search desperately for solutions, but few consider the most basic cause. Christ, however, went to the root of the matter. He said that envy, pride, impurity, immorality, theft, murder, and wickedness emanate from people's sinful hearts (Mark 7:20-23). People don't find solutions to many of their problems until they agree with God's diagnosis of the cause: personal sin.

Romans 3:23—The passage around this verse informs us that there is no distinction among people: Both Jews and Gentiles have sinned and fallen short of God's standard of righteousness. Everyone is in the same situation.

Note: Occasionally, in order to focus attention on a particular thought, you will memorize a verse that is not a complete sentence. This is another reason why you want to read the context of the verses as you begin to memorize them.

Isaiah 53:6 (recommended but optional)—Isaiah stated that everyone has willfully turned his or her back on God, preferring to remain independent from God. This is part of the natural human condition (Romans 3:10-12). Every person is infected and impacted by sin.

Your Weekly Plan

1. At the beginning of the week, check to see that you have your verse cards from books 1 and 2. Depending on what verses you chose to memorize, that would be between eleven and eighteen memory cards.

2. Each day review all the verses you have memorized during books 1 and 2.

3. From time to time, review the principles in "Proven Ways to Memorize a Verse Effectively" (page 24) in book 1.

4. A day or two before your next group session, write out your new verse(s) from memory or quote your verse(s) to someone, just to check accuracy.

WAYS TO MEDITATE ON SCRIPTURE: PART 2

In session 1, you applied the first two techniques for meditating on Scripture: paraphrase and questions. In this session, you'll experience four more approaches you can use for meditating on a Bible verse or passage.

3—Prayer

Pray over the verse or passage. One way to do this is to think about each phrase or thought and pray about the implications for your own life or the lives of others.

The best things I prayed about while meditating on Romans 12:1 were:

4—Emphasis

Emphasize different words or phrases. Read or quote a verse aloud several times and stress a different word or phrase each time. This alternates your focus on various facets of a verse. Each word adds its own significance to the passage.

The best thoughts I had while emphasizing different words in John 15:7 were:

5—Cross-Reference

Find cross-references. Using a concordance or other Bible study aid, find additional verses that support the basic concept of the passage you are cross-referencing. Two other verses that say some of the same things as John 14:21 are:

Reference: ____________ Thought: ____________

Reference: ____________ Thought: ____________

6—*Application*

Seek to make an application. Prayerfully reflect on the passage, allowing God to show you how to apply its truths. Try to make your application a positive, specific step you will take.

In considering how Philippians 4:6-7 relates to my own circumstances, I had the following thoughts:

INTRODUCTION TO BIBLE STUDY—BOOK 3

Having completed books 1 and 2 in The 2:7 Series undoubtedly deepened your convictions about the value of searching Scripture and clarifying truth. You have probably noticed that when you investigate the Word for yourself, it affects your attitudes and actions day after day.

However, even though you realize the importance of systematic Bible study, you will probably sense opposition as you continue. The enemy of every Christian, Satan himself, knows the power of God's Word, and he will try at every turn to keep you from it. You will find such excuses as "I'm too busy" or "I can't concentrate now—I'll do this little thing first and then get back to Bible study." You will find interruptions, temptations, and even criticism by others hindering you from giving your attention to Scripture.

Recognizing that Satan is the cause of many hindrances is helpful. It underscores the importance of Bible study and can deepen our resolve to ensure time for study. How do we win these encounters? Here are some practical, helpful suggestions.

1. Accept by faith that Christ has already won over Satan and his demonic compatriots. "Thanks be to God! He gives us the victory through our

Lord Jesus Christ" (1 Corinthians 15:57).

2. Ask the Lord for wisdom, insight, and strength. "Call to me and I will answer you and tell you great and unsearchable things you do not know" (Jeremiah 33:3).
3. Use personal discipline. No spiritual exercise becomes automatic. Just as you take the initiative to keep up your daily quiet time with the Lord, so you need to plan and zealously guard your study time. It is good to set a definite goal for a certain amount of study to be completed each week and be diligent in reaching that goal. Solomon said, "A longing fulfilled is sweet to the soul" (Proverbs 13:19), and reaching a planned objective brings satisfaction and further motivation.
4. Ask a friend to check you on your weekly Bible study progress. Perhaps mutually share what you have each studied.

Your Bible studies in book 3 are related to Christian character. One definition of character is "moral excellence and firmness." It is doing what God says even though it may be hard. God desires that we have strong, moral qualities in our inner lives as well as acceptable and effective outward behavior. Therefore, it is imperative that we learn what God's Word says about the character of the Christian. The five areas of Christian character your group will study in this course are:

- The Call to Fruitful Living
- Love in Action
- Purity of Life
- Integrity in Living
- Character in Action

ASSIGNMENT FOR SESSION 3

1. Scripture Memory: Study and complete "Scripture Memory Guide—Week 3" (pages 27–28). Memorize the verse(s) on "Sin's Penalty": Romans 6:23 and Hebrews 9:27 (recommended but optional).
2. Quiet Time: Continue reading, marking, responding back to God in prayer, recording on *My Reading Highlights*, and using a prayer sheet.
3. Bible Study: Complete the Bible study "The Call to Fruitful Living" (pages 28–35).
4. Evangelism: Perhaps you will be one of those to tell "My Story" in class with or without notes in less than four minutes.

SESSION 3

OUTLINE OF THIS SESSION

1. Open the session in prayer.
2. Break into verse review groups and quote the verse(s) on "Sin's Penalty": Romans 6:23 and Hebrews 9:27 (recommended but optional). Work at getting anything signed that you can on *My Completion Record.* If you are able to memorize more than the required verse(s), get sign-off on those as well.
3. Share some quiet-time thoughts from *My Reading Highlights.*
4. Listen to two or three people tell their "My Story" with or without notes in less than four minutes.
5. Discuss the Bible study "The Call to Fruitful Living" (pages 28–35).
6. Read "Assignment for Session 4" (page 35).
7. Have a short period of group prayer for some of those on your evangelism prayer lists.

SCRIPTURE MEMORY GUIDE—WEEK 3

About the Verses

TOPIC 2: SIN'S PENALTY

The fact that every person is a sinner has serious consequences.

Romans 6:23—Paul says that spiritual death is the result of sin. Spiritual death is separation from God. All will die physically some day, but all have already died spiritually. There are many people who believe in the existence of God but have no personal relationship with Him. They may be unaware that an impassable gulf separates them from God because of their sin.

God is love, but He is also just. He cannot overlook sin and still remain both just and holy. The only thing a holy God can do to sin is judge it. The Bible says, "Whoever rejects the Son will not see life, for God's wrath remains on him [literally, 'hangs over his head']" (John 3:36). We might not like to think about it, but the Bible speaks as much about judgment as it does of almost any other topic. We need to know about it.

Hebrews 9:27 (recommended but optional)—Every person has an appointment with physical death, but those without Christ die and then have to give account of themselves to God, their Judge. Christians will not face this judgment for their sins (John 5:24).

Your Weekly Plan

1. At the beginning of the week, have your cards ready for reviewing your memorized verses from books 1 and 2.

2. Each day review all your book 3 verses and verses memorized during books 1 and 2.

3. A day or two before your next group session, write out your new verse(s) from memory or quote your verse(s) to someone, just to check accuracy.

THE CALL TO FRUITFUL LIVING

Many people measure the fruitfulness of their lives by the quantity of their activities. This does not necessarily give a true picture of the quality of their lives. Who we are is more important than what we do.

THINK ABOUT:

How do you think fruitfulness should be measured in the life of a Christian?

GOD'S DESIRE FOR YOUR FRUITFULNESS

1. Read John 15:5. Here Christ gives essential insight into the matter of spiritual fruit-bearing.

   a. In this analogy, identify the vine and the branches.

   b. What condition is necessary for the branch to bear fruit?

   c. Why does the branch need the vine?

   d. Explain what you think it means to "abide" or "remain" in Christ.

2. From John 15:8 and 16, what additional observations can you make about bearing fruit?

3. Read Galatians 5:22-23 and list the qualities that God wants to produce in your life. Briefly define each one.

THE FRUIT OF THE SPIRIT	BRIEF DEFINITION OF THE FRUIT
1.	
2.	
3.	
4.	
5.	
6.	
7.	
8.	
9.	

Which of these qualities is currently the most important to you and why?

GROWING IN CHARACTER

4. Scripture reveals several important areas of life in which character is displayed. Please list one for each of the following verses.

   Philippians 4:8

   Colossians 4:6

   1 Peter 2:12

   How do these areas relate to one another?

5. Carefully examine 2 Peter 1:1-8. This portion of Scripture deals with the subject of growth in Christian character.

   a. How has God equipped you to grow in character (verses 2-4)?

   b. What does verse 8 say about fruitfulness?

c. List eight aspects of Christian character (verses 5-7).

How might their sequence be significant?

d. From 2 Peter 1:5-7, choose three of the eight qualities and write your own definition for each.

1.

2.

3.

e. Select one quality you would like to strengthen. With God's help, what steps could you take to become more Christlike in displaying that quality?

Sow a thought, reap an act;
Sow an act, reap a habit;
Sow a habit, reap a character;
Sow a character, reap a destiny.

—Unknown

GROWING IN WISDOM

6. One of the purposes of the book of Proverbs is that people might attain wisdom. What do the following verses from Proverbs teach about wisdom?

   2:6 ______

   3:13-14 ______

   9:10 ______

   11:2 ______

   24:13-14 ______

7. Read James 3:13-18.

   a. How is godly wisdom displayed? ______

   b. List the characteristics of godly wisdom and ungodly wisdom (verses 15-17). (You may leave some lines blank.)

GODLY WISDOM	UNGODLY WISDOM

   c. Which of the characteristics you listed have influenced our society the most? Please briefly explain your answer.

Wisdom is more than knowledge, which is the accumulation of facts. . . . It is the right application of knowledge in moral and spiritual matters.

—J. OSWALD SANDERS

CHANGING ATTITUDES

8. Read Philippians 3:4-14.

a. List several of Paul's new attitudes and patterns that differed from his former ones.

PAUL'S FORMER ATTITUDES AND PATTERNS (Verses 4-7)	PAUL'S NEW ATTITUDES AND PATTERNS (Verses 7-14)
1. Put confidence in the flesh	______
2. Religious leader	______
3. Persecuted the church	______
4. Blameless in the law	______
5. Counted all as gain for self	______

b. Why do you feel that Paul had such a positive attitude about the future? ______

9. In the Sermon on the Mount, Jesus Christ gave eight basic ingredients for living a holy, happy life. From Matthew 5:3-12, please list the blessing that He promised to the person with each quality.

KIND OF PERSON	JESUS' PROMISE
a. The poor in spirit (recognizing one's own poverty in spiritual things) (verse 3)	______
b. A person who mourns (is genuinely sorry for sin) (verse 4)	______

KIND OF PERSON	JESUS' PROMISE
c. The meek (having strength under control) (verse 5)	
d. A person who hungers for righteousness (deep concern for holiness) (verse 6)	
e. The merciful (compassionate toward others) (verse 7)	
f. The pure in heart (free from moral sin) (verse 8)	
g. The peacemaker (promotes peace by reconciling others) (verse 9)	
h. The persecuted (oppressed for Christ's sake) (verses 10-11)	

10. In which one of the eight areas are you currently the strongest? ______

    In which one would you like to see improvement? ______

SUMMARY

Review the following chapter subtopics and write your own summary of each section.

God's Desire for Your Fruitfulness

Growing in Character

Growing in Wisdom

Changing Attitudes

ASSIGNMENT FOR SESSION 4

1. Scripture Memory: Study and complete "Scripture Memory Guide—Week 4" (pages 37–38). Memorize the verse(s) on "Christ Paid the Penalty": Romans 5:8 and 1 Peter 3:18 (recommended but optional).
2. Quiet Time: Continue reading, marking, responding back to God in prayer, recording on *My Reading Highlights*, and using a prayer sheet.
3. Bible Study: Complete the Bible study "Relationship Evangelism" (pages 38–41).
4. Evangelism: Perhaps you will be one of those to tell "My Story" in class with or without notes in less than four minutes.

SESSION 4

OUTLINE OF THIS SESSION

1. Open the session in prayer.
2. Break into verse review groups and quote the verse(s) on "Christ Paid the Penalty": Romans 5:8 and 1 Peter 3:18 (recommended but optional). Work at getting anything signed off that you can on *My Completion Record*. If you are able to memorize more than the required verse(s), get sign-off on those as well.
3. Share some quiet-time thoughts from *My Reading Highlights*.
4. Listen to those who still need to tell their "My Story" with or without notes in less than four minutes.
5. Discuss the Bible study "Relationship Evangelism" (pages 38–41).
6. Read "Assignment for Session 5" (page 41).
7. Close the session in prayer.

SCRIPTURE MEMORY GUIDE—WEEK 4

About the Verses

TOPIC 3: CHRIST PAID THE PENALTY

Either we must suffer the punishment for our sins and be separated from God throughout eternity, or someone else must pay the penalty so we can go free. Only Jesus Christ—the sinless, perfect God-man—could do this for us.

Romans 5:8—Paul said that God showed His great love for us by sending Christ to die in our place, even while we were still undeserving sinners. This is pure love and grace.

1 Peter 3:18 (recommended but optional)—Peter told why Christ, the Righteous One, died for us, the unrighteous ones. He did it "to bring us to God"—to bridge the gulf that separated us from God's presence and prevented our having a personal relationship with Him.

On the cross, God placed our sins on His Son. Jesus Christ bore our penalty, which is separation from the Father. That is why Jesus cried out "My God, my God, why have you forsaken me?" (Matthew 27:46). The Father turned away from His Son because in that moment He was made sin for us. Now, instead of our sins, we have Christ's righteousness imparted to us and we can enter the very presence of God.

Your Weekly Plan

1. Remember, always say the topic first, then the reference, the verse, and the reference again at the end.

2. Each day review all your book 3 verses and verses memorized during books 1 and 2.

3. A day or two before your next group session, write out your new verse(s) from memory or quote your verse(s) to someone, just to check accuracy.

RELATIONSHIP EVANGELISM

TWO KEY INGREDIENTS

Scripture gives us insight into how the gospel can have its greatest impact. There are two key ingredients: telling (or proclaiming) the gospel and affirming (or modeling) the gospel message through the life of a believer. This study will help you understand the scriptural basis for proclaiming and modeling the message.

PROCLAIMING THE GOSPEL

1. According to 2 Corinthians 5:18-20, with what have we as Christians been entrusted? ____________________

2. In Mark 16:15, what are Christians commanded to do? ____________________

3. In Ephesians 3:7-8, what does Paul see as his life purpose? ____________________

4. Based on the verses in questions 1–3, please briefly state the Christian's responsibility in proclaiming the gospel. ____________________

In addition to proclaiming the gospel, the Christian is directed to affirm or display the reality of the Christian message in his or her own life. In this manner, a person on the way to believing the gospel not only hears but also sees what it means to have a relationship with Jesus Christ.

AFFIRMING THE GOSPEL

5. How does Christ instruct us to relate to the non-Christians around us (Matthew 5:13-16)?

6. According to Philippians 2:14-15, how do our lives function in affirming the gospel?

7. From the following verses, list some of the ways we are to relate to unbelievers:

   Matthew 5:43-48

   Luke 14:12-14

   Colossians 4:5-6

   2 Corinthians 4:5

   How do those actions and attitudes affirm the gospel?

8. From Matthew 9:10-13, explain how Jesus Christ related to unbelievers and what His purpose was.

9. Why is friendship with a person necessary for affirming the gospel?

> "My food," said Jesus, "is to do the will of him who sent me and to finish his work. Do you not say, 'Four months more and then the harvest'? I tell you, open your eyes and look at the fields! They are ripe for harvest. Even now the reaper draws his wages, even now he harvests the crop for eternal life, so that the sower and the reaper may be glad together. Thus the saying 'One sows and another reaps' is true. I sent you to reap what you have not worked for. Others have done the hard work, and you have reaped the benefits of their labor."
>
> —JOHN 4:34-38

In the John 4 passage, seeing people come to Christ is equated with reaping a harvest; it is the final step in a series of activities. A harvest must be preceded by breaking up ground, sowing, watering, growing, and, finally, reaping. Christ tells us that when we are involved in reaping (seeing someone come to Christ), much preliminary labor has already been done by others.

10. Before coming to Christ, what are some similar ways that planting, watering, and growing might take place in a non-Christian's life (John 4:34-38)? ______

11. In 1 Corinthians 3:5-9, Paul describes a real example of how planting, watering, and growing took place.
    a. What does verse 8 say about teamwork that moves people toward Christ? ______
    b. Who or what causes gospel truth (planted in minds) to grow (verses 6-7)? ______

c. What is the individual Christian's responsibility (verses 5,8-9)?

SUMMARY

The Christian has been provided with two primary means to win the world to Christ: the message of the gospel and the reality of the gospel in the Christian's life. These two means are effective in reaching both the religious and the secular person. Relationship evangelism is primarily the process of adapting the two means to the best advantage for the person we are seeking to lead to Christ. Relationship evangelism is a process, and its length will be determined to a great extent by how much or how little labor has been done before we enter into the picture with that individual. Nevertheless, the ultimate results of evangelism are dependent upon God who "gives the growth" and the individual who must, through an act of his or her will, repent and voluntarily receive Christ as Savior and Lord.

ASSIGNMENT FOR SESSION 5

1. Scripture Memory: Study and complete "Scripture Memory Guide—Week 5" (pages 43–44). Memorize the verse(s) on "Salvation Not by Works": Ephesians 2:8-9 and Titus 3:5 (recommended but optional).
2. Quiet Time: Continue reading, marking, responding back to God in prayer, recording on *My Reading Highlights*, and using a prayer sheet.
3. Bible Study: Complete the Bible study "Love in Action" (pages 44–49).
4. Evangelism: Do you still need to tell "My Story" with or without notes in less than four minutes?

SESSION 5

OUTLINE OF THIS SESSION

1. Open the session in prayer.
2. Break into verse review groups and quote the verse(s) on "Salvation Not by Works": Ephesians 2:8-9 and Titus 3:5 (recommended but optional).
3. Share some quiet-time thoughts from *My Reading Highlights.*
4. Listen to those who still need to tell their "My Story" with or without notes in less than four minutes.
5. Discuss the Bible study "Love in Action" (pages 44–49).
6. Read "Assignment for Session 6" (page 50).
7. Close the session in prayer.

SCRIPTURE MEMORY GUIDE—WEEK 5

About the Verses

TOPIC 4: SALVATION NOT BY WORKS

Many people have the idea that their eternal destiny will be decided by their good deeds being weighed against their bad ones, so they try to earn or solicit God's mercy by good and charitable acts in hopes of blinding God to their shortcomings and moral failures.

Ephesians 2:8-9—Paul made it clear that salvation is not by our works but only by God's grace. Through Christ we receive undeserved and unmerited favor. Salvation is a gift we receive by faith. If we were able to earn our salvation, we could boast in that accomplishment. But God alone must receive the credit for saving us.

Titus 3:5 (recommended but optional)—Here again, Paul states that we are not saved by our own efforts but by God's merciful action. This is hard for some people to accept. It goes against a person's independent nature and "do it yourself" philosophy of life. To be saved means we are cleansed of our sins and spiritually born anew. This is a work of the Holy Spirit, who causes regeneration in us. He cleanses and renews us from the inside out.

Your Weekly Plan

1. Read the context of your new verse(s) in your Bible to help you clarify the setting.

2. Each day review all your book 3 verses as well as verses memorized during books 1 and 2.

3. Strive for word perfection. A day or two before your next group session, write out your new verse(s) from memory or quote your verse(s) to someone, just to check accuracy.

LOVE IN ACTION

In our twenty-first-century world, people have many different definitions of love. Many of these come from the illustrations of love found in movies, on television, in advertisements, online, and, perhaps, from personal experience. The Scriptures speak directly about love. The Bible tells us what love is and how we may demonstrate it.

THINK ABOUT:

Generally what is the world's concept of love?

WHAT IS GENUINE LOVE?

1. How is love defined?
    a. What are some dictionary definitions for love that reflect a secular viewpoint? ________

    b. How does a Bible dictionary define love? ________

    c. How do the two differ? ________

2. From 1 Corinthians 13:4-8, list some of the characteristics of *agape* love.

WHAT LOVE IS	WHAT LOVE IS NOT

Based on this passage, what are two or three major conclusions you can make about love?

3. Carefully read 1 John 4:8-21.

a. What important fact about God do you see in verses 8 and 16?

b. What has God done to demonstrate His love for us?

c. Because of God's love for us, what should our response be (verses 11,19)?

d. To what degree can love and fear exist together (verse 18)?

THE FOCUS OF YOUR LOVE

4. From the passages you have studied, how would you define love in your own words?

5. Read John 13:34-35.
   a. What is one of the surest evidences that you are a follower of Christ?

   b. Why do you think Jesus placed such emphasis on demonstrating love?

Love enters into everyday actions in a variety of ways. Many people relate to others with only the tacit agreement "If you do your part, I'll do mine." This conditional way of giving of ourselves is not love. God wants us to say, "I'll love you even if I receive nothing in return." It is this selfless giving and loving that God wants developed in our attitudes and actions.

LOVE IN HUMILITY

6. Humility comes from having the right perspective about God and ourselves. What do the following verses tell us about our perspective toward God and ourselves?

   Jeremiah 9:23-24

   Philippians 2:3-4

7. Read 1 Peter 5:5-6.

   a. What does the passage teach about humility? ______

   b. Why do you think God places such a high value on humility in a person's life? ______

8. Consider Romans 12:3.

   a. What error must we be careful to avoid? ______

   b. What are the results of overestimating ourselves? ______

   c. What are the results of underestimating ourselves? ______

PRIDE

Thinking too highly of self: "God's work can't get along without me!	Thinking too lowly of self: "God can't do anything through me!"

Both situations in this illustration are manifestations of pride because the person is preoccupied with self.

9. Summarize the relationship between love and humility. ______

LOVE IN SPEECH AND ACTION

10. Read Colossians 4:6 and write a paraphrase of it.

11. God can give you gracious and loving words. According to the following verses, what can the right words do?

    Proverbs 12:25

    Proverbs 15:23

    Proverbs 16:24

    Proverbs 23:16

    Love is not merely an inner feeling but also an act of the will. Love can be known by only the action it produces.

12. Read 1 John 3:16-18. Indicate how love can be demonstrated toward others.

13. List some practical ways you personally can demonstrate love toward Christians and non-Christians.

    Christians

    Non-Christians

To love the whole world
For me is no chore;
My only real problem's
My neighbor next door.

—Unknown

SUMMARY

Review the chapter subtopics and write your own summary of each section.

What Is Genuine Love?

The Focus of Your Love

Love in Humility

Love in Speech and Action

ASSIGNMENT FOR SESSION 6

1. Scripture Memory: Study and complete "Scripture Memory Guide—Week 6" (pages 51–52). Memorize the verse(s) on "Must Receive Christ": John 1:12 and Romans 10:9-10 (recommended but optional).
2. Quiet Time: Continue reading, marking, responding back to God in prayer, recording on *My Reading Highlights*, and using a prayer sheet.
3. Bible study: Complete the Bible study "Purity of Life" (pages 52–58).
4. Evangelism: Listen to those who still need to tell their "My Story" with or without notes in less than four minutes.

SESSION 6

OUTLINE OF THIS SESSION

1. Open the session in prayer.
2. Break into verse review groups and quote the verse(s) on "Must Receive Christ": John 1:12 and Romans 10:9-10 (recommended but optional).
3. Share quiet-time thoughts from *My Reading Highlights*.
4. Listen to those who still need to tell their "My Story" with or without notes in less than four minutes.
5. Discuss the Bible study "Purity of Life" (pages 52–58).
6. Read "Assignment for Session 7" (page 58).
7. Close the session in prayer.

SCRIPTURE MEMORY GUIDE—WEEK 6

About the Verses

TOPIC 5: MUST RECEIVE CHRIST

The New Testament teaches that we are saved solely by believing in Jesus Christ; nothing else is required. Today, *believe* often means merely to give mental assent. Many say, "Oh yes, I believe in God." But in the Bible, belief means completely trusting and resolutely committing oneself to Jesus Christ as Savior from sin. Paul wrote, "In the gospel a righteousness from God is revealed, a righteousness that is by faith from first to last" (Romans 1:17). When we have faith that Christ died for us personally, we show our belief by placing our full trust in Christ's sacrifice on the cross for us. We turn away from our sin, receive Christ, and accept the gift of eternal life. Your memory work for this week stresses the importance of both believing (shown by action) and verbalizing that belief.

John 1:12—John equated receiving Jesus Christ with believing in Him. This is how one becomes a child of God. Everyone is familiar with the act of receiving a gift. One simply takes it, thanks the person who gave it, and then enjoys the gift.

Romans 10:9-10 (recommended but optional)—There is a point in time when a person comes to know and believe the gospel. He or she understands the substitutionary death of Christ on the cross, the forgiveness of sin, and Christ's rightful ownership over one's life. A person realizes in his or her heart and mind, "I now understand what Christ did on the cross and I know He died for me."

It is important for a person to confirm his or her faith in Christ by verbally acknowledging Him as Savior and Lord. A way to do this is to thank God in prayer for forgiveness and eternal life through Christ and then state clearly to another Christian that he or she has believed in and accepted Christ's gospel. There may be dangerous family or cultural situations that make it unsafe to share with anyone but a Christian.

Your Weekly Plan

1. By now you may be motivated to begin learning your new verse(s) the very first day after your class.

2. Each day review all your book 3 verses as well as verses memorized during books 1 and 2.

3. Before your next group session, write out your new verse(s) from memory or quote your verse(s) to someone, just to check accuracy.

PURITY OF LIFE

It has been stated, "The new morality is nothing more than the old immorality in modern clothes." As society experiences moral decline, it becomes less popular for the Christian to take a stand on the moral absolutes of God's Word. Though freedom from all moral responsibility is sought by many people, Christians will find God's greatest blessing only by continuing to live by the principles and guidelines of God's Word.

THINK ABOUT:

Generally what does the world use as standards for evaluating morality?

GOD'S STANDARD

1. What is God's standard for purity (1 Peter 1:15-16)? ____________

How do you think God expects us to live up to this standard? ____________

2. According to the following verses, what are some ways we can (with God's help) exhibit His standard?

   Matthew 5:21-22 ____________________

   Matthew 5:27-28 ____________________

   Romans 12:1-2 ____________________

   2 Corinthians 7:1 ____________________

> Every man has a train of thought on which he rides when he is alone. The dignity and nobility of his life, as well as his happiness, depend upon the direction in which that train is going, the baggage it carries, and the scenery through which it travels.
>
> —Joseph Fort Newton

3. Study Colossians 1:21-23.

   a. What has God done to ensure our holiness? ____________________

   b. What must we do? ____________________

THE IMPORTANCE OF PERSONAL PURITY

4. Read 1 Corinthians 6:12-20.

   a. List several reasons why we should avoid immorality. ____________________

b. How do you think immoral behavior affects our relationship with God? ___

c. How does it affect our relationship with others? (Consider both Christians and non-Christians.)

5. The world's standards differ greatly from God's. From 1 John 2:15-16, what are three characteristics in people that reflect the world's standards? Please list and define these below.

CHARACTERISTIC	DEFINITION
1.	
2.	
3.	

6. What do the Scriptures say to the following excuses for wrong moral behavior?

a. "Since everyone else does it, it must be right."

Proverbs 14:12 ___

b. "I need to discover only what is right for me."
Ecclesiastes 11:9 ___

c. "Nobody will ever find out that I did it."

Hebrews 4:13 ___

d. "I'll stop after this one time."

Galatians 6:7-8 ______

e. "I didn't really do anything; all I did was think it."

Matthew 5:28 ______

7. The battle for purity is found in the mind. Read Romans 8:5-8.

a. What two types of people are referred to in the passage? ______

b. What are the results of each mind-set? ______

THE PATH TO PURITY

8. On what should we choose to focus our thoughts (Philippians 4:8)?

Suggest some practical ways to motivate yourself to dwell on these things. ______

Try to forget the number 13. When you have forgotten it, check this box: ☐ This is how some people try to avoid immorality—they think they can just make themselves not think about it. It is impossible to eliminate a wrong thought from your mind unless you substitute something good in its place. How might memorizing and meditating on Scripture safeguard your thought life?

9. Read Ephesians 4:17-24.
   a. How does the passage describe the non-Christian's lifestyle?

   b. What steps should Christians take to overcome their former way of life (verses 22-24)?

   c. What are some practical ways to do this?

10. According to the following verses, what can we do to live a clean life, pleasing to the Lord?

    Psalm 119:9-11

    Proverbs 4:14-15

    Romans 13:14

    Galatians 5:16

11. Study Genesis 39:7-12 and 2 Samuel 11:1-4. Compare the events in Joseph's and David's lives.
    a. What were the surrounding circumstances?

JOSEPH	DAVID

b. What were their respective attitudes?

JOSEPH	DAVID

c. What were their resulting actions?

JOSEPH	DAVID

d. Why do you think these two men responded in different ways to a similar situation?

12. What scriptural standards do you have concerning your relationship with the opposite sex? Please state two of them and what verses they're based on.

> Food was meant for the stomach and the stomach for food; but God has no permanent purpose for either. But you cannot say that our physical body was made for sexual promiscuity; it was made for the Lord, and the Lord is the answer to our deepest longings.
>
> —1 CORINTHIANS 6:13 (PH)

SUMMARY

Review the following chapter subtopics and write your own summary of each section.

God's Standard

The Importance of Personal Purity

The Path to Purity

ASSIGNMENT FOR SESSION 7

1. Scripture Memory: Study and complete "Scripture Memory Guide—Week 7" (pages 59–60). Memorize the verse(s) on "Assurance of Salvation": 1 John 5:13 and John 5:24 (recommended but optional).
2. Quiet Time: Continue reading, marking, responding back to God in prayer, recording on *My Reading Highlights*, and using a prayer sheet.
3. Evangelism:
   a. Do you still need to tell "My Story" with or without notes in less than four minutes?
   b. Read the material on The Bridge Illustration (pages 60–70) and be prepared to discuss it with your group.

SESSION 7

OUTLINE OF THIS SESSION

1. Open the session in prayer.
2. Break into verse review groups and quote the verse(s) on "Assurance of Salvation": 1 John 5:13 and John 5:24 (recommended but optional).
3. Share some quiet-time thoughts from *My Reading Highlights*.
4. Listen to those who still need to tell their "My Story" with or without notes in less than four minutes.
5. Discuss The Bridge Illustration (pages 60–70).
6. Read "Assignment for Session 8" (page 70).
7. Close the session in prayer.

SCRIPTURE MEMORY GUIDE—WEEK 7

About the Verses

TOPIC 6:

ASSURANCE OF SALVATION

It is nearly impossible to build a solid structure on a shaky foundation. And it is very difficult to grow in the Christian life properly if one is unsure of his or her salvation. Some Christians do not believe they can know they have eternal life. Others gauge the assurance of their salvation by their feelings, a most unstable foundation. But God wants us to *know* we have eternal life.

1 John 5:13—John stated clearly that his primary objective in this epistle was to help those who believe in Jesus Christ to know they have eternal life. But how can we know? One evidence is our desire to please God, resulting from the Holy Spirit's residence in our bodies. Other evidences of new life in Christ are the desires to read His Word, commune with Him in prayer, fellowship with other believers, and tell others about Christ. But the foundation on which all evidence rests is the promise of God's Word.

John 5:24 (recommended but optional)—Jesus said that if we hear His Word and believe in the Father through Christ, we have eternal life. This eternal life is a *present* possession. We will never have to face judgment for our sins because the moment we believe, we pass from spiritual death to spiritual life. The primary basis for assurance of salvation is to believe what God says about it—what He has promised.

Your Weekly Plan

1. During your daily review, give special attention to your newest memory verses. Don't rush through the review. Think about the meaning and implications of the verses for your own life.

2. Use spare moments during the day for memorizing and review. Small segments of time each day can enable you to review all the verses you have memorized in books 1–3 in THE 2:7 SERIES.

3. At the end of the week, write out your new verse(s) from memory or quote your verse(s) to someone else, just to check accuracy.

THE BRIDGE ILLUSTRATION

HOW TO USE THE BRIDGE ILLUSTRATION TO COMMUNICATE THE GOSPEL

The Bridge Illustration is one of many effective methods for presenting the gospel. It has been used successfully to communicate the gospel over many years and in many contexts, in groups and person to person. You will find it a useful and powerful tool for explaining the gospel.

Many variations of The Bridge Illustration are in use. The presentation described here is relatively simple and straightforward. Your group leader might ask you to make adjustments to the format presented here in your workbook. Learn the method he or she presents, and become skilled in that method. After you have used this method to present the gospel to several people, you may want to make a few adjustments in the format to make it more your own. This illustration will become a sharpened tool in your hands if these adjustments are based on experience in communicating the gospel to actual people.

FLEXIBILITY

The Bridge Illustration can take as little as ten minutes to present, or it can be stretched out to an hour or more. A normal presentation will last fifteen to thirty minutes. The flexibility of this presentation is one of its greatest assets. It can be tailored specifically to a person or situation.

SENSITIVITY

The way in which the Holy Spirit leads you to witness will vary in different situations. It is important to be observant and sensitive as you relate to the person with whom you are sharing The Bridge. In any type of ministry situation, it is important to pray silently and ask God for guidance, wisdom, and the ability to communicate the gospel clearly.

THE LEAD-IN

Experience has shown that it is helpful to have a few statements and questions in mind to help open the door for presenting the gospel. If you haven't spoken much about spiritual matters, you might say, "We're all on a spiritual journey. Where would you say you are in that journey?" Often an ideal time to share the gospel is after a person has heard a salvation story—yours or someone else's. You first want to get that person's response to the salvation story he or she has heard by saying something like "Well, that's my story. What do you think?" Or "Well, you just heard her story. What is your reaction to what happened to her?" A more direct lead-in is "How about you, Pat? Have you ever thought much about what it takes to go to heaven?"

If there is time to talk further and the person shows interest and a capacity to hear more, you might say something like "You know, Jim, there's an illustration that summarizes and clarifies what it means to become a real Christian and know with certainty that you have eternal life. If you have a few minutes, may I sketch it out for you?" If he says yes, you may proceed.

If you feel that the person has heard as much as he or she can absorb at the time, you might say something like "You know, Pat, there's a diagram that clarifies what it means to be a real Christian and know for certain that you have eternal life. When you have fifteen or twenty minutes sometime, why don't we sit down and I will sketch it out for you, okay?" Then at a later, appropriate time, you can ask permission to go through the illustration.

In many situations, you will find it natural to ask permission to draw out the illustration without having shared your salvation story.

PRESENTATION

One of the most effective ways to present the gospel using The Bridge Illustration is to ask questions about Scripture that will enable a person to see each truth directly from the Bible. You will need to convey four concepts as you draw out The Bridge:

1. God's Purpose	Abundant Life (John 10:10)
	Eternal Life (John 3:16)
2. Our Problem	All Have Sinned (Romans 3:23; Isaiah 53:6)
	Sin's Penalty (Romans 6:23; Hebrews 9:27)
3. God's Remedy	Christ Paid the Penalty (Romans 5:8; 1 Peter 3:18)
	Salvation Not by Works (Ephesians 2:8-9; Titus 3:5)
4. Our Response	Must Receive Christ (John 1:12; Romans 10:9-10)
	Assurance of Salvation (John 5:24; 1 John 5:13)

Usually you will use only one verse from each of the four topics as you present the gospel.

The diagrams on pages 63–66 show how your illustration will develop as you present it. The printed text shows how you can use questions to present this material. You should note that each segment is introduced by a transition statement, followed by one or more questions. After the person has had a chance to state his or her observations, clarify and summarize each point and make the transition to the next Scripture passage.

> We are therefore Christ's ambassadors, as though God were making his appeal through us. We implore you on Christ's behalf: Be reconciled to God. (2 Corinthians 5:20)

> But in your hearts set apart Christ as Lord. Always be prepared to give an answer to everyone who asks you to give the reason for the hope that you have. But do this with gentleness and respect. (1 Peter 3:15)

DIALOGUE: **GOD'S PURPOSE**

"Let's look at two Bible verses that tell us about some of what God wants for us."

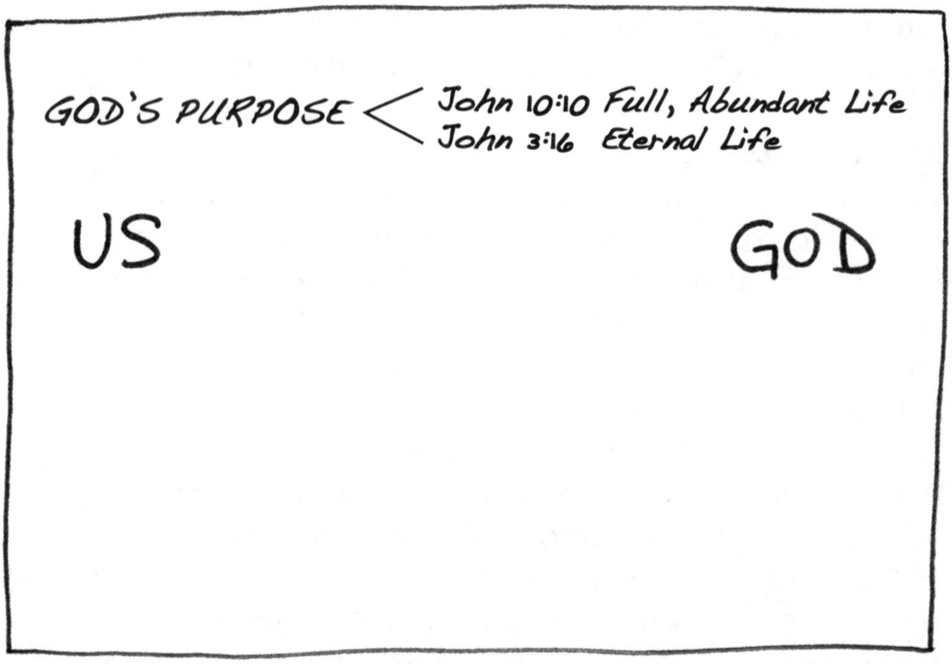

John 10:10
Question: "What does this passage say is one of God's reasons for sending His Son?"

Transition: **"God wants us to experience a full, abundant life. This would include such things as love, peace, purpose, and fulfillment."**

John 3:16
Question: "What additional reason do you see for God sending His Son?"

Transition: **"So, then, from these statements we can say that God wants us to experience a full, abundant life now and eternal life both in this life and after death."**

DIALOGUE: **OUR PROBLEM**

Comment: "But we have a problem. God did not create us as His robots—to love God and to automatically live perfect lives. God gave us a will and the freedom of choice. Our sins separate us from Him."

Romans 3:23
Question: "What does this verse say about all people? Does this include me? Does this include you? How would you describe sin according to this verse?"

Transition: **"Have you ever wondered what effect our sin has? Let's look at another passage."**

Hebrews 9:27
Question: "What is one thing death brings with it?"

Comment: "You can see by this statement that each of us will die physically, and after we die physically we will face judgment."

Romans 6:23
Question: "How would you define *wages*?"

Transition: **"So, we see that we have sinned and there are eternal consequences for our sins. God provides a wonderful remedy for our problem if we have humility enough to accept it."**

DIALOGUE: **GOD'S REMEDY**

Comment: "In spite of the fact that we have turned our backs on God and have disobeyed Him, He has provided a remedy so that we can know Him personally. He wants to give us both full, abundant life and eternal life. Only one bridge can cross the gulf that exists between a person and God, and that bridge is Jesus Christ, through His death on the cross."

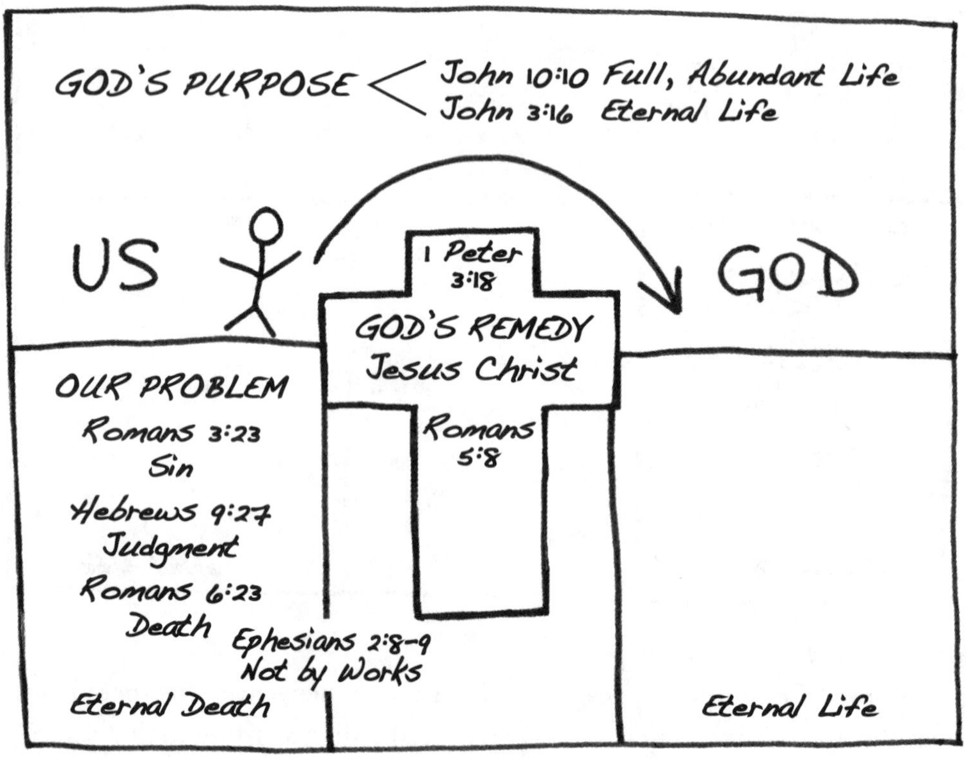

Romans 5:8
Question: "Did God want us to become worthy before He provided a solution? What did God do?"

Transition: **"People use many approaches in trying to find favor with God and secure eternal life."**

Ephesians 2:8-9
Question: "What does the Bible say about the relationship between salvation and our efforts to be good? What is one reason God won't accept our good deeds as payment for our sins?"

(You may or may not choose to use 1 Peter 3:18. It is a powerful summary verse and an excellent verse to emphasize the good news of Christ's resurrection.)

Transition: **"Let's look at what our response might be to God's remedy."**

DIALOGUE: **OUR RESPONSE**

Comment: "Real belief results in a response on our part. Christ has made it possible for us to cross over to God's side and experience the full life He wants us to have. But we are not automatically on God's side."

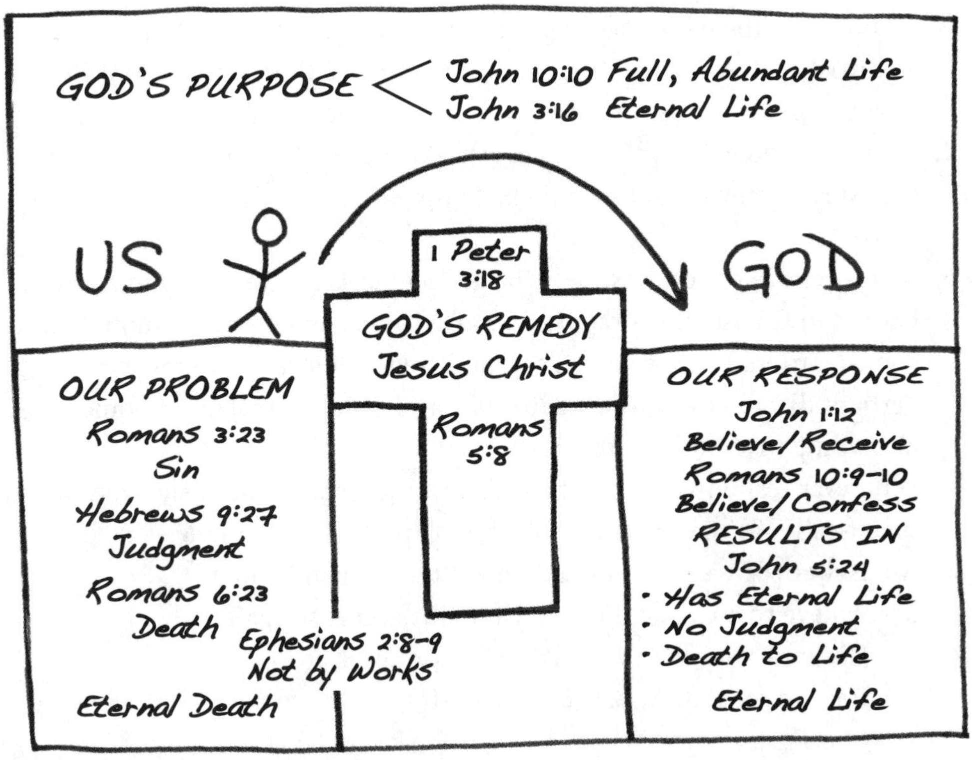

John 1:12

Question: "What does this passage equate with believing? What does receiving Christ mean to you? (At this point, you might clarify that believing and receiving involve our mind, our emotions, and our will.)

Comment: "God does not want us to wonder if we have eternal life; He wants us to be certain. The Bible says, 'I write these things to you who believe in the name of the Son of God so that you may know that you have eternal life' (1 John 5:13)."

PERSONAL INVITATION

Assume that you have been sharing the gospel with Susan. You might use some of the following suggestions to help her move toward a personal commitment:

1. "Does this make sense to you?"
2. "Do you have any questions about it?"
3. "Where would you place yourself in this illustration?"
   a. If Susan says, "On God's side," you might ask, "On what basis do you believe that you are going to heaven? (Her answer tells you where she is—maybe on the bridge, not over it).
   b. If she points to the left side or to the bridge, inquire, "What would you have to believe or do to be on God's side?" See if she can clearly communicate the issues of the gospel and the necessity of believing in Christ and receiving Him. You might say, "Is there any reason why you shouldn't cross over to God's side and be certain of eternal life?"
4. If she is responsive to the gospel, ask, "Would you like to receive Jesus Christ right now? If so, I would be happy to pray with you and help you do that."
5. If you believe she understands the gospel but is not yet ready to commit her life to Christ, encourage her to give these things further thought and consideration. Be sure she takes The Bridge Illustration home with her. Perhaps discuss the gospel again later and get her involved in some type of investigative Bible study.
6. Whatever response she has, be sure she understands what she would specifically pray to affirm her faith in Christ. It is as simple as A, B, C:
   A—Acknowledge your sin and be willing to turn from it.
   B—Believe that Christ died for your sins and rose again.
   C—Commit your life to Christ as Savior and Lord.

   You can see that A, B, C corresponds to Our Problem, God's Remedy, and Our Response.

PRACTICAL SUGGESTIONS

1. Do not memorize The Bridge Illustration. Learn the principles, ideas, verses, and key sentences. Make it your own.
2. Make an outline of the presentation as you would like to give it, and practice giving it by yourself.
3. Draw the illustration as you talk and listen.
4. Use a Bible rather than quoting verses. Have the non-Christian read the verses aloud from a Bible.
5. If the non-Christian brings up objections during your presentation, you might say, "That's a good question. For the sake of continuity, may I try to answer that after completing the illustration?"
6. The ultimate goal is to bring a person to salvation in Christ. Proceed as far as the Holy Spirit gives you freedom. If the non-Christian is open to receiving Christ, help him or her pray to receive Christ.

In this course as you present The Bridge, you are not expected to use all of the interactive questions that are provided for you. In session 8, you draw out The Bridge outline. This means the visual things—the words, the cliffs, the cross, and the Bible references. In sessions 9 and 10, you draw out The Bridge as you verbally explain it. You will want to practice alone in preparation for those two presentations.

SAMPLE: HOW YOUR TWO PRESENTATIONS MIGHT SOUND

It is not required, but if you have time, you are welcome to learn some of the questions and transitional statements suggested in this chapter. After this course, you may want to set aside time to learn the questions and transitional statements and put them in your own words.

Following is a sample of what your "lecture" type of presentation might resemble when you give it to one of your classmates in sessions 9 and 10. (Ask your classmate to read each of the verses aloud, but he or she should not ask questions or interact with you. For a change of pace, you might read a verse here and there.) As you think of the meaning of each verse and learn the sequence for drawing The Bridge, you will probably make a better presentation than this following brief sample:

First let's look at a couple of verses that explain what **God's Purpose** is for you and me. Let's look at the book of John, chapter 10 and verse 10. [The verse is read aloud.] As you can see, it says that God wants us to have a full, abundant, quality kind of life. He really wants the best for us. Let's read John 3:16. [The verse is read aloud.] So, you see in John 3:16 that God also wants us to have eternal life so we can live with Him after this life.

Next we look at **Our Problem**. We need to see the bad news side of our situation before we look at the good news side.

One question is why so many people are not experiencing the full life God wants for them. Let's look at Romans 3:23. [The verse is read aloud.] We see that I have sinned and you have sinned. Every person in the world has done things morally wrong in God's eyes, to various degrees. Let's read Hebrews 9:27. [The verse is read aloud.] This verse says that we will all die physically and then face God as our judge. Now let's read Romans 6:23. [The verse is read aloud.] The payment for our sins is eternal death or separation from God.

But God has provided a wonderful remedy (**God's Remedy**) for our terrible dilemma. Let's look at Romans 5:8. [The verse is read aloud.] It is incredible, but Christ died in our place. He took the penalty for our sins Himself on the cross.

Now let's look at Ephesians 2:8-9. [The verse is read aloud.] Many people believe that God is keeping score of what we do, whether right or wrong—that when we die, God adds up the scores. If we have done more good than bad, we get to go to heaven. You can see in Ephesians 2:8-9 that eternal life is a gift. Romans 6:23, which we looked at earlier, also said that eternal life is a gift. We can't work for a gift. If we work for it, then it is wages. You can see here in Ephesians 2 that salvation and eternal life do not come to us through our good deeds.

Finally, we need to look at **Our Response**. Eternal life is a free gift, but each person must reach out and receive or accept that free gift—to embrace it by faith. Everybody doesn't automatically have the gift of eternal life, but we can ask for eternal life based on an understanding of Christ's death on the cross for us.

Let's read John 1:12. [The verse is read aloud.] John 1:12 says that when anyone reaches out and receives Christ into his or her heart (or inner life), that person becomes a child of God in a new and very special way.

Let's look at Romans 10:9-10. [The verse is read aloud.] Do you believe the things we've seen in these several verses? Do you believe them down in your heart as it says here in Romans 10? God would love to hear you say to Him out loud that you believe them. I suggest that in a few minutes we say a simple prayer to God and let Him know that you believe these things and that you want Christ to come into the center of your life.

But let's look at one final summary verse. It's wonderful! Look at John 5:24. [The verse is read aloud.] You see it says that if a person hears these things we're talking about and if that person genuinely believes them in his or her heart, three things happen. First, that person has eternal life right then and there. Second, that person will never have to stand before God, as Judge, and face severe consequences. And, third, that person passes from the eternal death side over to the eternal life side.

I suggest that we have a "make sure" prayer—that we say a prayer to God and let Him hear from your own lips that you understand and believe what Christ has done for you. Then ask Christ to come into your heart and life to apply His death on the cross for you for the forgiveness of your sins. Ask Him to take over your life, give you the gift of eternal life, and help you become all He wants you to be and help you do whatever He wants you to do. Tell Him that you are turning away from your sins and that you want to live a new life, close to Him, as He helps you do that. Thank Him for Jesus Christ. Finish by saying, "Amen."

Please keep in mind that this is a sample. When you explain The Bridge, do it in a way that is clear and logical to you. Both the contents of the presentation and the suggested prayer are highly adaptable. Be sure your explanation of The Bridge and the prayer of commitment contain all the essential elements.

Come to session 8 ready to draw out The Bridge outline—everything that is visual. Then, in the following weeks, you will present The Bridge in a "lecture" form as illustrated in the sample we just went over. Make brief notes that you can refer to as you practice drawing the outline for The Bridge in preparation for session 8. Then you can make notes to use as you practice for the lecture presentations for sessions 9 and 10. The visual picture in mind helps you recall the sequence.

As a part of this course, you have memorized several of the verses you will use in The Bridge, but when you use The Bridge, it is better for you to have the verses read aloud rather than quoting them.

Paul was prepared to proclaim his faith:

> From morning till evening he explained and declared to them the kingdom of God and tried to convince them about Jesus from the Law of Moses and from the Prophets. Some were convinced by what he said, but others would not believe.
>
> —ACTS 28:23-24

ASSIGNMENT FOR SESSION 8

1. Scripture Memory: Review all the verses memorized in book 3.
2. Quiet Time: Continue reading, marking, responding back to God in prayer, recording on *My Reading Highlights*, and using a prayer sheet.
3. Bible Study: Complete the Bible study "Integrity in Living" (pages 71–75).
4. Evangelism:
   a. Prepare to draw the outline (verses and main points) of The Bridge Illustration for another member of your class.
   b. Do you still need to tell "My Story" in class with or without notes in less than four minutes?

SESSION 8

OUTLINE OF THIS SESSION

1. Open the session in prayer.
2. Break into verse review groups and work on getting anything signed that you can on *My Completion Record.*
3. Share some quiet-time thoughts from *My Reading Highlights.*
4. Listen to those who still need to tell their "My Story" with or without notes in less than four minutes.
5. Discuss the progress you are making with non-Christians.
6. Break into groups of two and take turns presenting The Bridge Illustration outline.
7. Discuss the Bible study "Integrity in Living" (pages 71–75).
8. Read "Assignment for Session 9" (page 76).
9. Close the session in prayer.

INTEGRITY IN LIVING

Every day we deal with issues of right versus wrong, good versus evil. When struggling with these issues, many people rationalize their behavior and disregard God's standards of integrity. Often these sins are explained away or ignored. They become the "vices of the virtuous"—sins that may have become accepted as the norm. As followers of Christ, we want to avoid compromises and subtle erosion in our character.

THINK ABOUT:

How would you define or describe *little white lies*?

THE STRUGGLE FOR INTEGRITY

One definition of *integrity* is "the quality or state of being of sound moral principles; uprightness, honesty, and sincerity."[1]

1. Describe the natural condition of our hearts (Jeremiah 17:9). ______

2. According to the following verses, what are some of the ways we can be deceived?

James 1:22 ______

1 John 1:8 ______

Romans 16:17-18 ______

Ephesians 4:14 ______

2 Corinthians 11:3-4 ______

3. Saul, the first king of Israel, is a good example of a man who lacked personal integrity. Please read 1 Samuel 15:1-23.

a. What was Saul commanded to do (verses 1-3)? ______

b. What did he do (verse 9)? ______

c. How did he try to justify his disobedience (verses 13-21)? ______

d. How did God view the situation (verses 22-23)? ______

4. Hypocrites pretend to be what they are not. Study Mark 7:6-8. Then list what Jesus says about hypocrites and give an example of each.

THE HYPOCRITE	EXAMPLE

LIVING A LIFE OF INTEGRITY

5. Read 1 Thessalonians 2:3-11. How did the apostle Paul demonstrate a life of integrity?

   a. By speech

   b. By deed

   c. Through motives

6. Read 1 Timothy 3:1-9.

   a. Which qualities required for a person seeking church office have to do with integrity?

   b. Are these qualities only for church leaders or for all Christian to attain? Explain.

7. List the qualities of a person of integrity from Psalm 15:1-5.

Which of these qualities do you think are most violated among the people with whom you associate? Consider both believers and non-believers. ______

8. Integrity needs to be displayed in all aspects of our lives.
   a. Using the following verses, list some of the areas where integrity tends to be neglected.

      Romans 13:6-7 ______

      Ephesians 5:22 ______

      Ephesians 5:25 ______

      Ephesians 6:1-2 ______

      Colossians 3:23-24 ______

      1 Peter 2:13-14 ______
   b. Is there ever a time when integrity toward God would override our commitment to these areas of responsibility (Acts 4:18-20 and 5:27-29)?

THE CONSCIENCE: AN AID TO INTEGRITY

9. How does a dictionary define *conscience*? ______

10. Using the following passages, describe the conscience.

    1 Corinthians 8:7-12 ______

    1 Timothy 3:9 ______

    1 Timothy 4:2 ______

    Titus 1:15 ______

    Hebrews 10:22 ______

1 Peter 3:16,21 ______

11. Read Acts 24:16.

a. What were Paul's objectives regarding his conscience? ______

b. How can we develop or maintain this kind of conscience?

Toward God ______

Toward people ______

SUMMARY

Review the following chapter subtopics and write your own summary of each section.

The Struggle for Integrity

Living a Life of Integrity

The Conscience: An Aid to Integrity

ASSIGNMENT FOR SESSION 9

1. Scripture Memory: Work on any requirements not yet completed.
2. Quiet Time: Continue reading, marking, responding back to God in prayer, recording on *My Reading Highlights*, and using a prayer sheet.
3. Evangelism:
   a. Prepare to draw out and explain The Bridge Illustration to another member of your class. (This is "Lecture Presentation 1.")
   b. Do you still need to tell "My Story" with or without notes in less than four minutes?
4. Other:
   a. Study and complete "Verse Analysis of Matthew 6:33" (pages 77–80).
   b. Study and complete "Priorities: Part 1" (pages 80–84).

SESSION 9

OUTLINE OF THIS SESSION

1. Open the session in prayer.
2. Break into verse review groups and work on getting anything signed that you can on *My Completion Record*.
3. Share some quiet-time thoughts from *My Reading Highlights*.
4. In groups of two, take turns drawing and explaining The Bridge Illustration.
5. Listen to those who still need to tell their "My Story" with or without notes in less than four minutes.
6. Discuss "Verse Analysis of Matthew 6:33" (pages 77–80).
7. Discuss "Priorities: Part 1" (pages 80–84).
8. Read "Assignment for Session 10" (page 84).
9. Close in prayer with a focus on priorities.

VERSE ANALYSIS OF MATTHEW 6:33

PREPARATION FOR DISCUSSING PRIORITIES

This study is foundational for the discussion on priorities in sessions 9 and 10. After reading the context of Matthew 6:33 aloud twice, take the following steps to analyze it:

1. Paraphrase the verse.
2. Study the context.
3. Find cross-references.
4. Write down real or potential problems.
5. Make a personal application.

☐ I have read Matthew 6:19-34 aloud twice. (Please check when completed.)

1. **PARAPHRASE**
   Paraphrase Matthew 6:33 in your own words. You may want to refer to the following Bible versions as part of your paraphrasing process:

But seek first his kingdom and his righteousness, and all these things will be given to you as well. (NIV)

But seek first the kingdom of God and His righteousness, and all these things shall be added to you. (NKJV)

But seek first the kingdom of God and his righteousness, and all these things will be added to you. (ESV)

And he will give you all you need from day to day if you live for him and make the Kingdom of God your primary concern. (NLT)

Steep your life in God-reality, God-initiative, God-provisions. Don't worry about missing out. You'll find all your everyday human concerns will be met. (MSG)

But seek (aim at and strive after) first of all His kingdom, and His righteousness (His way of doing and being right), and then all these things taken together will be given you besides. (AMP)

2. **CONTEXT**
   Summarize the key thoughts in Matthew 6, verses 25-32 and 34. Do not include verse 33.

3. **CROSS-REFERENCES**

How are the following verses similar to Matthew 6:33?

Deuteronomy 28:2

2 Chronicles 26:5

2 Chronicles 31:20-21

Psalm 84:11

4. **PROBLEMS**

a. Define righteousness and kingdom of God in the following spaces. You will want to use a dictionary, Bible dictionary, encyclopedia, or commentary in preparing your definitions. You can also find excellent resources online.

Righteousness

Kingdom of God

b. What does the word *seek* imply?

c. This verse opens up with the word *but*. Compare verse 33 with verses 31-32. What contrast does the word *but* imply?

5. APPLICATION

What is one application of Matthew 6:33 that you can make to your own life?

PRIORITIES: PART 1

Priorities have to do with order and importance. A priority list includes things in the order of their importance.

Why do we feel that one thing is more important than another? It depends on what we want and what we would like to accomplish—what our goals and desires are. We all have goals and desires, and these influence our choices.

A Christian's priorities should be based on God's will for his or her life as revealed in Scripture. Jesus Christ gave us the injunction "But seek first his kingdom and his righteousness" (Matthew 6:33). That which pertains to God's kingdom has priority over our physical needs, according to the context of the Sermon on the Mount.

To have the right priorities, we need to have the right goals. From the following verses, write the goals and desires these godly men had or exhorted others to have.

David (Psalm 27:4)

Joshua (Joshua 24:15)

Jesus (John 4:34)

Paul (Romans 12:2)

Paul (Colossians 1:28-29)

John (3 John 4) ______

______

As committed Christians, we want to follow their example: "Remember your leaders, who spoke the word of God to you. Consider the outcome of their way of life and imitate their faith" (Hebrews 13:7).

GOALS

The goals for our lives, on which our priorities should be based, can be divided into two areas: what we are to be (growing in Christlikeness [Romans 8:29]), and what we are to do (growing in effective service [Galatians 6:9-10]).

Christlikeness

From the following passages, make a list of the characteristics of Christlikeness, using a translation, not a paraphrase:

GALATIANS 5:22-23	MATTHEW 5:3-10
1. ______	1. ______
2. ______	2. ______
3. ______	3. ______
4. ______	4. ______
5. ______	5. ______
6. ______	6. ______
7. ______	7. ______
8. ______	8. ______
9. ______	

From the two lists, what do you feel are the five most important characteristics of Christlikeness?

1. ______
2. ______
3. ______
4. ______
5. ______

Serving

Serving means helping at the point of need. This may mean offering aid or advice; it could also mean admonishing a friend, sharing the gospel, or helping someone memorize Scripture.

There are many ways in which we might serve others. Please match each of these eight service activities to its corresponding Scripture reference.

______	Mark 9:41	1. Doing humble tasks for God's children
______	John 13:14-16	2. Caring for widows
______	Acts 6:1-3	3. Helping meet material or financial needs
______	Ephesians 4:12	4. Praying for others
______	Ephesians 6:5-7	5. Building up other Christians
______	Colossians 4:12	6. Being thorough and hardworking on the job
______	1 Timothy 5:17	7. Giving a drink of cold water
______	1 John 3:17-18	8. Preaching and teaching the Word of God

The greatest service you can render to people is to bring them into a right relationship with Jesus Christ. This could be helping someone come to salvation in Christ or ministering to the spiritual development of a Christian.

"Seeking the kingdom of God first" has to do with glorifying God in the lives of individuals, so our highest concern in serving Christ is to minister to spiritual needs and then to other needs people have. At times it might be necessary to minister to material or physical needs before we can minister to spiritual needs.

GUIDELINES FOR SETTING AND APPLYING PRIORITIES

1. **Make responsible choices**. Many of life's choices are already made for us: by Scripture (God), parents, government, and physical limitations. But whenever we have options, we are responsible to make choices. Slaves had little power of choice, yet in the first century, the gospel spread rapidly among them. Do you want to have a life that makes a difference—that matters for eternity? Run for the prize (1 Corinthians 9:24).
2. **Be decisive**. One of the greatest hindrances to doing God's will is a lack of planning. Most of us have a number of unplanned hours each week to use any way we wish. As we prayerfully make our plans, we want to keep Matthew 6:33 in mind. For example, how will you plan to use a free evening or a Saturday or Sunday afternoon?

3. **Plan ahead**. The following approach can sharpen your effectiveness:
   a. Make one list of things you need to do, and another list of things you would like to do.
   b. Pray for sensitivity from the Holy Spirit as you evaluate the things on your lists.
   c. Number the items in the order of their importance.
   d. From your "need to do" list, do item 1. Then do item 2 and so on through your list.
   e. From time to time, slip into your "need to do" list something from your "would like to do" list. An occasional change of pace can be refreshing!
   f. Keep revising your lists to accommodate new demands and opportunities. Many people make a new list every morning or the night before.
4. **Persevere**. Determination and perseverance are two important ingredients for living according to priorities. Our flesh may rebel against our doing what we need to do. Paul said, "I beat my body and make it my slave" (1 Corinthians 9:27). In other words, he is saying, "I make my body do what it should be doing, not what it wants to do."
5. **Acknowledge dependence on God**. While we know that determination and perseverance contribute to success with priorities, we also want to recognize that God gives blessing and grace, making our efforts really count (see 2 Corinthians 3:5; John 15:5; Zechariah 4:6). Depend on God's enablement.
6. **Be adaptable**. In the book of James, we are taught that when we have made our plans, we must learn to say, "If it is the Lord's will, we will live and do this or that" (4:13-16). Sometimes we are unaware of God's plans for us. His thoughts are higher than our thoughts (see Isaiah 55:9); we don't want to get bent out of shape when interruptions come but rather submit to God with thanksgiving in all our circumstances (see Romans 8:28; Psalm 115:3).
7. **Don't be easily swayed**. Sometimes people try to control our lives. At one point in Christ's ministry, people were trying to make plans for Him (see Luke 4:42-44), but He would not submit to them. He said He had to do what His Father sent Him to do. Knowing what God wants us to do helps us decide when to go along with the desires of well-meaning people and when graciously to say no.
8. **Review your goals**. We want to align both our personal goals and our daily choices with God's purposes as revealed in Scripture. Human nature tends to lead us away from our goals. A half day alone with God

regularly is an excellent activity for helping maintain direction, motivation, and a sense of priority.

9. **Prioritize**. Working by priority does not mean you will get everything done that you would like to. It does mean you will get the most important things done. Jesus said, "I have brought you [God the Father] glory on earth by completing the work you gave me to do" (John 17:4), yet there was much more He could have done. Let us learn from Jesus' example and live by God's priorities for our lives and commit to Him the things we are unable to do.

CONCLUSION

Sometimes priorities are based on selfish desires. The flesh tends to make it difficult for us to relate our priorities to God's plan for our lives because doing so sometimes involves sacrifice.

Do you want God to be first in your life? If so, work on His purposes and priorities as a lifelong process. Don't be discouraged when you fall short; instead, make periodic evaluations, such as regularly spending an extended time in prayer and planning.

> And he will give you all you need from day to day if you live for him and make the Kingdom of God your primary concerrn. (Matthew 6:33, NLT)

ASSIGNMENT FOR SESSION 10

1. Scripture Memory: Continue reviewing your verses and work on any requirements not yet completed.
2. Quiet Time: Continue reading, marking, responding back to God in prayer, recording on *My Reading Highlights*, and using a prayer sheet.
3. Evangelism:
   a. Prepare to draw out and explain The Bridge to another member of your class. (This is "Lecture Presentation 2.")
   b. Do you still need to tell "My Story" with or without notes in less than four minutes?
4. Other: Read and be prepared to discuss "Priorities: Part 2" (pages 85–90).

SESSION 10

OUTLINE OF THIS SESSION

1. Open the session in prayer.
2. Break into verse review groups and work on getting anything signed that you can on *My Completion Record*.
3. Share some quiet-time thoughts from *My Reading Highlights*.
4. Listen to those who still need to tell their "My Story" with or without notes in less than four minutes.
5. In groups of two, draw and explain The Bridge Illustration to each other.
6. Discuss "Priorities: Part 2" (pages 85–90).
7. Read "Assignment for Session 11" (page 90).
8. Close the session in prayer.

PRIORITIES: PART 2

THE PRIORITY OF GOD

> I want you to live as free of complications as possible. When you're unmarried, you're free to concentrate on simply pleasing the Master. Marriage involves you in all the nuts and bolts of domestic life and in wanting to please your spouse, leading to so many more demands on your attention. The time and energy that married people spend on caring for and nurturing each other, the unmarried can spend in becoming whole and holy instruments of God.
>
> —1 Corinthians 7:32-33 (MSG)

For every Christian man or woman, whether single or married, God needs to be the first priority. E. M. Bounds's classic statement "To be little with God is to be little for God" captures the idea of this priority. We spend time with God because He greatly desires our fellowship. He longs to be with us, for we are "the kind of worshipers the Father seeks" (John 4:23). In His presence, we grow in godliness, and the reality of our relationship with God becomes apparent to those around us. Acts 4:13 says, "When they saw the courage of Peter and John and realized that they were unschooled, ordinary men, they were astonished and they took note that these men had been with Jesus."

Occasionally, larger blocks of time with God can supplement your regular devotional times. You can develop an amazingly practical working knowledge of the Bible through Scripture memory and Bible study. Pray regularly for God to give you wisdom in applying the Word to your life. If you have a grasp on the great truths of the Bible, you will frequently find yourself in places of effective ministry. Over time, your life will touch the lives of many. The triangle diagram shows that the closer two individuals are to God, the closer they will be to each other. This is true between husband and wife, between parent and child, between any two Christians. Therefore, as you pursue God, you will reap relational benefits as well as personal benefits. Continue to put your walk with God first! "As for me, it is good to be near God. I have made the Sovereign LORD my refuge" (Psalm 73:28). "The LORD is near to all who call on him, to all who call on him in truth. He fulfills the desires of those who fear him" (Psalm 145:18-19).

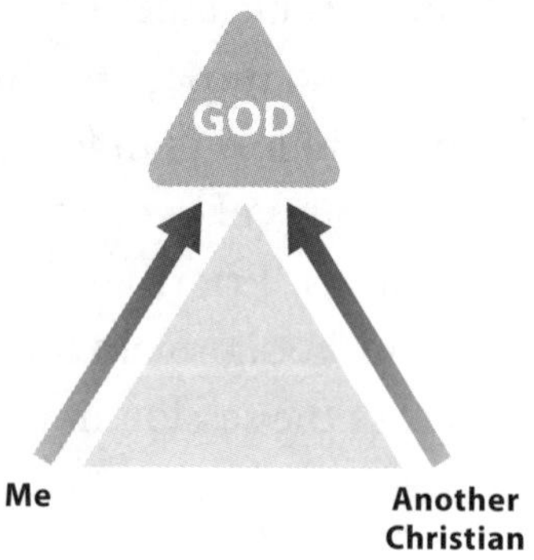

CIRCLES OF PRIORITY

The following illustration, the Circles of Priority, is a visual representation of our common responsibilities in life. The inner circles are the higher priorities, yet we want to move toward balance in all areas at the various stages of our lives.

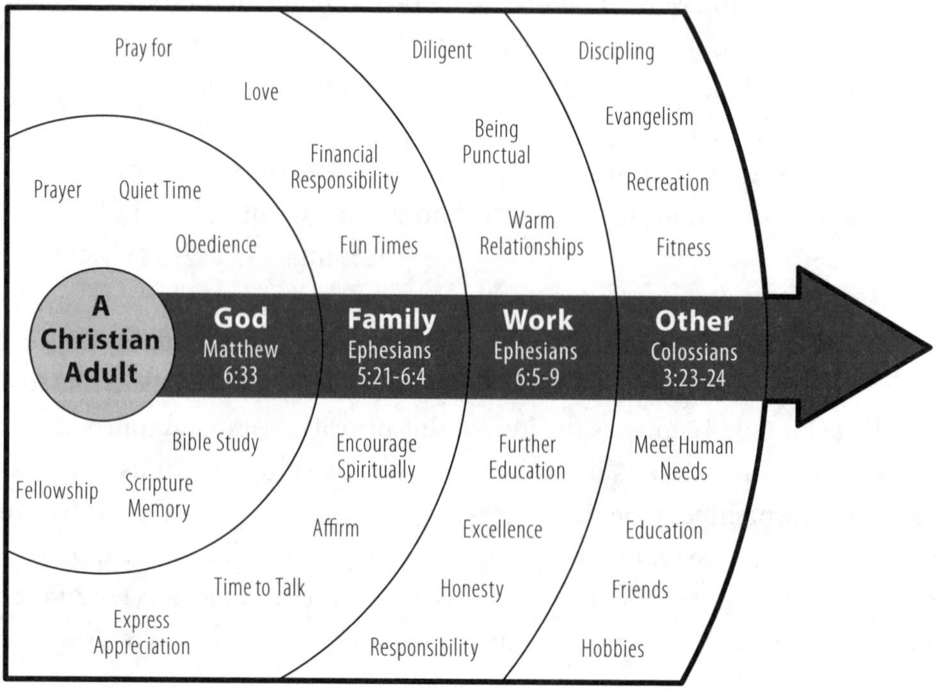

God has given each of us basic responsibilities we must not neglect. Ultimately, you will determine in your own heart and mind what is a priority for you in a given week or on a given day. We want to give high-priority tasks and relationships extra weight when planning and scheduling our time. Before we can be significantly effective for Christ, we need to spend consistent, meaningful time with God. He is to be our first priority (Matthew 6:33). In fact, He is our priority of priorities! "He has showed you, O man, what is good. And what does the LORD require of you? To act justly and to love mercy and to walk humbly with your God" (Micah 6:8).

THE PRIORITY OF FAMILY

The best springboard for a great influence for Christ in the lives of many people may be simply sharing the biblical principles that work in your marriage or in raising your children. Credibility in the family needs to precede expansion of spiritual influence. First Timothy 3:5 says, "If anyone does not know how to manage his own family, how can he take care of God's church?" Not that we need to have everything in order in every dimension of our family life, but we need to give a high priority to getting our own house in order. Our home will become either a springboard to greater ministry or a hindrance to it.

> For I have chosen him, so that he will direct his children and his household after him to keep the way of the LORD by doing what is right and just, so that the LORD will bring about for Abraham what he has promised him. (Genesis 18:19)

Because of Abraham's faithfulness in the management of his family, God prospered him in other ways.

Husband or Wife

Having a close vital relationship with God increases the probability of having a close vital relationship with your spouse. And having a good relationship in your marriage increases the probability of having a good relationship with your child. Priority does not imply neglect; it implies emphasis. Continue to work on your marriage.

Wives. Are you praying for your husband? Are you helping him to become more and more the leader and decision maker he should be? Are you adapting to him? Are you a student of your husband, learning his moods, likes and dislikes, and strengths and weaknesses? Do you support and encourage him in what he feels led to pursue in life?

Husbands. Are you praying for your wife? Are you lifting your share of the load in household responsibilities and with the children? Have you recently read a book, listened to a CD, or watched a DVD to sharpen your parenting skills? Are you and your wife thinking and planning together? Would your wife say you talk and pray together often enough? How often do you say thank you? Are you helping to meet your wife's spiritual, physical, and emotional needs as well as the financial ones?

You will have your greatest effectiveness in furthering the purposes of God in the world if you put your relationship with God first and your spouse a strong second.

Children

Whether you are married or find yourself in a situation of being a single parent, you will agree that your children are unbelievable blessings as well as incredible responsibilities. However, we live in a most opportune time in history. The Christian sector has a proliferation of books, CDs, website resources, DVDs, and seminars on how to raise children. Many pastors and Christian counselors are experienced and trained to assist us through some of the more difficult struggles. We need to allot time for acquiring the necessary knowledge and skills and to have the courage to seek sound advice or counseling when needed.

We want to avoid bypassing our children for "the ministry." We may find that we have not prepared our children for the opportunities and difficulties of life or helped them become disciples of Jesus Christ. At times, for the sake of our children, we may need to decrease our involvement in ministry, realizing that our own children represent a very high ministry priority.

Single Adults

If you are a single adult, you have special benefits and advantages that enable you to make a significant contribution to what God desires to accomplish in the world today. A large segment of the adult population is single. Single people are often more mobile and flexible in regard to where they can live and what they can do. They often have more time than married people for Bible intake and spiritual growth. Personal and career development pursuits are also valuable. But this kind of time availability may not be true for those who are single parents or starting a business.

How much further education should you pursue? How much time should you spend with friends, neighbors, and roommates? What kind of ministry load can you carry that still leaves you time off for recreation and rejuvenation? God can lead you, so you want to make these issues a matter of prayer and give them adequate time for planning and evaluation.

Invest your single life wisely! Become all that God wants you to be, using the leverage of your situation to make an impact for Christ. God may lead you to get married one day, or He may be best able to work in and through you if you remain single. Follow Christ wholeheartedly. You can entrust your future to Him.

THE PRIORITY OF WORK

Your job may take up many hours each week, but it is a place where you can use your God-given skills and abilities. It supplies funds that can be invested to further the cause of Jesus Christ, as well as finances to meet your personal and family needs.

The workplace gives you a point of contact and friendship with a number of non-Christians who may come to Christ and become disciples. Of course, you want to touch lives spiritually without using "company time." As you work "heartily, as to the Lord" (Colossians 3:23, NKJV), your example gives you a platform for ministering to people and enhances your career as well.

THE PRIORITY OF CHURCH

Being a part of a local assembly of believers is most important. It is a place for both spiritual intake and ministry output. Teaching a class of adults, young people, or children can be both a ministry and a context within which you can grow in your ability to motivate others and communicate biblical truth clearly.

There are numerous opportunities to grow and minister. Pray for God's leading. Plan to be both taking in and giving out as you meet with other followers of Christ each week.

MINISTRY AND OTHER PRIORITIES

In books 1–3, there has been a persistent emphasis on the importance of relating to non-Christians, identifying with Christ, and then sharing your salvation story and the gospel. Ministry should be an integral part of the lifestyle of every believer if we hope to impact the world significantly for Christ. An increasing number of biblically sound churches are seeing the importance of ministering to physical and emotional needs as well as spiritual needs. There are limitless possibilities of ministry for every layperson. Some of the finest traditional and innovative ministries are being carried out by people who are not on the staff of a local church. They are "regular" Christians with jobs and perhaps homes and families. Plan to invest a portion of your energy in spreading the gospel, helping people become disciples, and meeting human needs.

Are you reading books, listening to podcasts or CDs, and enjoying a hobby? These are activities that can help make us sharper and more interesting to be around. Could further education perhaps help make you more effective in your job? Are you attending Christian or job-related seminars and conferences when they are available? We don't want to hit a plateau in life somewhere in our thirties, forties, or beyond.

Are you getting adequate exercise and sufficient time for rest and recreation? We want to give adequate attention to the care and welfare of our bodies and emotions as well as our spiritual lives and ministries.

ASSIGNMENT FOR SESSION 11

1. Scripture Memory: Work on getting any final memory verses signed off.
2. Quiet Time: Continue reading, marking, responding back to God in prayer, recording on *My Reading Highlights*, and using a prayer sheet.
3. Bible Study: Complete the Bible study "Character in Action" (pages 91–96).

SESSION 11

OUTLINE OF THIS SESSION

1. Open the session in prayer.
2. Break into verse review groups and work on getting anything signed that you can on *My Completion Record*.
3. Share some quiet-time thoughts from *My Reading Highlights*.
4. Discuss the Bible study "Character in Action" (pages 91–96).
5. Read aloud "Keep On Keeping On" (pages 97–98) to review what you have learned in *Bearing Fruit in God's Family* and in the first two books in The 2:7 Series.
6. Close the session in prayer.

CHARACTER IN ACTION

A Christian is not immune to the harsh realities of human life. Sickness, sorrow, death, and other forms of pain and suffering are experienced by all people. But for a Christian, trials and suffering carry with them the promise of God's loving presence and sovereign purpose in shaping the inner qualities of life.

THINK ABOUT:

Why do you think God allows Christians to experience trials and suffering?

GOD'S ULTIMATE CONTROL

1. Scripture tells us that God is all-powerful (omnipotent), all-knowing (omniscient), and present everywhere (omnipresent).
   a. Read Psalm 139:1-16 and summarize God's involvement with you in the following areas:
   God's knowledge of me (verses 1-6)

God's presence with me (verses 7-12)

b. What was the response of the psalmist to the knowledge of God's influence in his life?

Verses 17-18

Verses 23-24

2. What do the following verses teach about God's perspective and purpose?

Isaiah 45:5-7

Isaiah 46:9-10

Romans 8:28

TRIALS AND SUFFERING PRODUCE CHARACTER

3. Read James 1:2-4,12.

a. How should a person respond to trials?

b. What are the results of properly responding to trials?

4. In Romans 5:3-5, Paul says we are to exult (rejoice, glory) in our tribulations.

a. What does tribulation produce in the Christian life?

b. Is it significant that Paul mentioned these areas in a particular sequence? ______

5. How did the following men deal with adversity?

Joseph (Genesis 50:20) ______

Job (Job 1:13-22) ______

Shadrach, Meshach, Abednego (Daniel 3:13-18) ______

The Apostles (Acts 5:40-42) ______

Paul (Philippians 1:12-21) ______

What impresses you most from these examples? ______

6. What are some of the reasons God tested the people of Israel (Deuteronomy 8:1-3,16)?

RESPONSE TO TRIALS AND SUFFERING

7. Sometimes the suffering we go through is a result of God's discipline. Read Hebrews 12:4-11.

a. Why does God discipline us? ______

b. What are the results of God's discipline? ______

______

c. How can you tell the difference between being disciplined by God and an attack from Satan?

______

______

______

______

8. Though trials and suffering are difficult at the time, what are some positive aspects to consider?

Romans 8:18 ______

______

2 Corinthians 1:3-4 ______

______

1 Peter 5:10 ______

______

Can you think of other positive aspects of suffering? ______

______

______

9. Read Ephesians 5:20 and 1 Thessalonians 5:18.
   a. How does God want us to respond to every situation, including trials and suffering? ______

   ______

   ______

   b. Why do you think this response is important? ______

   ______

   ______

A person's positive response to problems contributes to his or her spiritual maturity. Each crisis is an opportunity for victory or defeat—for growth or decline.

10. Think back over a specific trial or suffering you have gone through and consider the following questions:

a. What was the trial or suffering? ______

b. How did you respond to it? ______

c. How could you have responded better? ______

d. Did you thank God for the circumstance? ______

e. How did God use it in your life? ______

f. Have you been able to use it to comfort someone else? ______

The truths in this old classic poem describe God's process with men and women alike:

When God wants to drill a man
And thrill a man
And skill a man.

When God wants to mold a man
To play the noblest part;
When He yearns with all His heart
To create so great and bold a man
That all the world shall be amazed,
Watch His methods, watch His ways!
How He ruthlessly perfects
Whom He royally elects!
How He hammers him and hurts him,
And with mighty blows converts him
Into trial shapes of clay which
Only God understands;
While his tortured heart is crying
And he lifts beseeching hands!
How He bends but never breaks
When his good He undertakes;
How He uses whom He chooses
And with every purpose fuses him;
By every act induces him
To try His splendor out—
God knows what He's about!

—Unknown

SUMMARY

Review the following chapter subtopics and write your own summary of each section.

God's Ultimate Control

Trials and Suffering Produce Character

Response to Trials and Suffering

KEEP ON KEEPING ON

WHAT YOU HAVE ACCOMPLISHED

Congratulations! You now have experienced the discipleship training in all three of the workbooks in THE 2:7 SERIES:

- *Growing Strong in God's Family*
- *Deepening Your Roots in God's Family*
- *Bearing Fruit in God's Family*

Your diligence has brought you through significant steps in your growth as a true disciple of Jesus Christ. Your Christian life and ministry have been enhanced by:

- Regularity in Scripture memory—you have now memorized at least seventeen verses
- Regularity in your quiet time—you are reading Scripture with an eye for marking, recording, and responding back to God in prayer
- Regularity in Bible study—you have completed seventeen topical question-and-answer Bible studies
- Presentation of your "My Story" (salvation story), which you have written out and are able to give in under four minutes
- Practicing explaining the gospel as you draw out The Bridge Illustration
- Praying conversationally, discussing how to spend extended time with God, and having participated in an extended time with God

- Being confronted with, submitting to, and living under the lordship of Christ
- Discussing ways to meditate on Scripture
- Discussing ways to recognize and set priorities in your life

Congratulations! You have persevered and made a wonderful investment in your own life!

> A desire fulfilled is sweet to the soul.
>
> —Proverbs 13:19 (ESV)

FREE CERTIFICATE OF COMPLETION

Your 2:7 group leader may download a certificate of completion for each person in your group. More information about the certificates is available at www.2-7series.org.

USE WHAT YOU KNOW—CONTINUE TO LEARN AND GROW

Graduation from high school appropriately has been called "commencement," meaning "a beginning" or "a start." There are young men and women in their twenties who are "old." There are people in their sixties who are "young." Decide to be a lifetime learner. Plan to have at least five quiet times each week and review your memory verses consistently. That kind of regularity produces great personal dividends. Blessings and Godspeed!

SPIRITUAL MULTIPLICATION

What is spiritual multiplication? It is spiritual parenting that leads to spiritual children, grandchildren, and great-grandchildren. Who do you know right now that you could help as a spiritual parent or as an "older brother" or "older sister" in Christ?

Over the months ahead, as you share your faith you will have your own spiritual children. Sometimes you will "adopt" a child or for a time be a "foster parent." Over the years, you can have children and grandchildren who live and spiritually reproduce in other cities and perhaps even in other countries. Your Christian life *can* impact the world!

A strong biblical precedent for multiplication is seen in the four generations of 2 Timothy 2:2: Paul, Timothy, dependable people, and others. Here you see parent, child, grandchildren, and great-grandchildren—spiritual multiplication!

> You and many others have heard what I have taught. You should teach the same thing to some people you can trust. Then they will be able to teach it to others.
>
> —2 TIMOTHY 2:2 (NCV)

If you have not yet read or listened to the message *Born to Reproduce*, plan to do that. You will find it online at www.discipleshiplibrary.com and at other websites. This classic message was given by Dawson Trotman, founder of The Navigators, at a conference sponsored by Back to the Bible in 1955. You will find other excellent resources to assist you in multiplying your Christian life at www.navpress.com, www.navigators.org/cdm, www.discipleshiplibrary.com, and www.2-7series.org.

APPENDIX

- My Reading Highlights
- Prayer Sheets

MY READING HIGHLIGHTS

"Now, my children, listen to me. Those who follow my ways are happy. Listen to my teaching, and you will be wise. Do not ignore it. Those who listen to me are happy. They stand watching at my door every day. They are at my open door waiting to be with me." —Proverbs 8:32-34 (NCV)

Translation ____________________ Year ________

☐ **Sunday** Date ____________ All I read today ____________

Best thing I marked today: *Reference* ____________

Thought: ____________

How it impressed me: ____________

☐ **Monday** Date ____________ All I read today ____________

Best thing I marked today: *Reference* ____________

Thought: ____________

How it impressed me: ____________

☐ **Tuesday** Date ____________ All I read today ____________

Best thing I marked today: *Reference* ____________

Thought: ____________

How it impressed me: ____________

☐ **Wednesday** Date ______________ All I read today ______________

Best thing I marked today: *Reference* ______________

Thought: ______________

How it impressed me: ______________

☐ **Thursday** Date ______________ All I read today ______________

Best thing I marked today: *Reference* ______________

Thought: ______________

How it impressed me: ______________

☐ **Friday** Date ______________ All I read today ______________

Best thing I marked today: *Reference* ______________

Thought: ______________

How it impressed me: ______________

☐ **Saturday** Date ______________ All I read today ______________

Best thing I marked today: *Reference* ______________

Thought: ______________

How it impressed me: ______________

MY READING HIGHLIGHTS

"Now, my children, listen to me. Those who follow my ways are happy. Listen to my teaching, and you will be wise. Do not ignore it. Those who listen to me are happy. They stand watching at my door every day. They are at my open door waiting to be with me." —Proverbs 8:32-34 (NCV)

Translation ______________________ Year __________

☐ **Sunday** Date ______________ All I read today ______________

Best thing I marked today: *Reference* ______________

Thought: ______________

How it impressed me: ______________

☐ **Monday** Date ______________ All I read today ______________

Best thing I marked today: *Reference* ______________

Thought: ______________

How it impressed me: ______________

☐ **Tuesday** Date ______________ All I read today ______________

Best thing I marked today: *Reference* ______________

Thought: ______________

How it impressed me: ______________

☐ **Wednesday** Date ______________ All I read today ______________

Best thing I marked today: *Reference* ______________

Thought: ______________

____

How it impressed me: ______________

____

____

____

☐ **Thursday** Date ______________ All I read today ______________

Best thing I marked today: *Reference* ______________

Thought: ______________

____

How it impressed me: ______________

____

____

____

____

☐ **Friday** Date ______________ All I read today ______________

Best thing I marked today: *Reference* ______________

Thought: ______________

____

How it impressed me: ______________

____

____

____

☐ **Saturday** Date ______________ All I read today ______________

Best thing I marked today: *Reference* ______________

Thought: ______________

____

How it impressed me: ______________

____

____

____

MY READING HIGHLIGHTS

"Now, my children, listen to me. Those who follow my ways are happy. Listen to my teaching, and you will be wise. Do not ignore it. Those who listen to me are happy. They stand watching at my door every day. They are at my open door waiting to be with me." —Proverbs 8:32-34 (NCV)

Translation ______________________ Year __________

☐ **Sunday** Date ______________ All I read today ______________

Best thing I marked today: *Reference* ______________

Thought: ______________

How it impressed me: ______________

☐ **Monday** Date ______________ All I read today ______________

Best thing I marked today: *Reference* ______________

Thought: ______________

How it impressed me: ______________

☐ **Tuesday** Date ______________ All I read today ______________

Best thing I marked today: *Reference* ______________

Thought: ______________

How it impressed me: ______________

☐ **Wednesday** Date __________ All I read today __________

Best thing I marked today: *Reference* __________

Thought: __________

How it impressed me: __________

☐ **Thursday** Date __________ All I read today __________

Best thing I marked today: *Reference* __________

Thought: __________

How it impressed me: __________

☐ **Friday** Date __________ All I read today __________

Best thing I marked today: *Reference* __________

Thought: __________

How it impressed me: __________

☐ **Saturday** Date __________ All I read today __________

Best thing I marked today: *Reference* __________

Thought: __________

How it impressed me: __________

MY READING HIGHLIGHTS

"Now, my children, listen to me. Those who follow my ways are happy. Listen to my teaching, and you will be wise. Do not ignore it. Those who listen to me are happy. They stand watching at my door every day. They are at my open door waiting to be with me." —Proverbs 8:32-34 (NCV)

Translation ______________________ Year __________

☐ **Sunday** Date ______________ All I read today ______________

Best thing I marked today: *Reference* ______________

Thought: ______________

____

How it impressed me: ______________

____

____

____

☐ **Monday** Date ______________ All I read today ______________

Best thing I marked today: *Reference* ______________

Thought: ______________

____

How it impressed me: ______________

____

____

____

____

☐ **Tuesday** Date ______________ All I read today ______________

Best thing I marked today: *Reference* ______________

Thought: ______________

____

How it impressed me: ______________

____

____

____

☐ **Wednesday** Date ____________ All I read today ____________

Best thing I marked today: *Reference* ____________

Thought: ____________

How it impressed me: ____________

☐ **Thursday** Date ____________ All I read today ____________

Best thing I marked today: *Reference* ____________

Thought: ____________

How it impressed me: ____________

☐ **Friday** Date ____________ All I read today ____________

Best thing I marked today: *Reference* ____________

Thought: ____________

How it impressed me: ____________

☐ **Saturday** Date ____________ All I read today ____________

Best thing I marked today: *Reference* ____________

Thought: ____________

How it impressed me: ____________

MY READING HIGHLIGHTS

"Now, my children, listen to me. Those who follow my ways are happy. Listen to my teaching, and you will be wise. Do not ignore it. Those who listen to me are happy. They stand watching at my door every day. They are at my open door waiting to be with me." —Proverbs 8:32-34 (NCV)

Translation ______________________ Year ________

☐ **Sunday** Date ______________ All I read today ______________

Best thing I marked today: *Reference* ______________

Thought: ______________

____

How it impressed me: ______________

____

____

____

☐ **Monday** Date ______________ All I read today ______________

Best thing I marked today: *Reference* ______________

Thought: ______________

____

How it impressed me: ______________

____

____

____

____

☐ **Tuesday** Date ______________ All I read today ______________

Best thing I marked today: *Reference* ______________

Thought: ______________

____

How it impressed me: ______________

____

____

____

☐ **Wednesday** Date ______________ All I read today ______________

Best thing I marked today: *Reference* ______________

Thought: ______________

How it impressed me: ______________

☐ **Thursday** Date ______________ All I read today ______________

Best thing I marked today: *Reference* ______________

Thought: ______________

How it impressed me: ______________

☐ **Friday** Date ______________ All I read today ______________

Best thing I marked today: *Reference* ______________

Thought: ______________

How it impressed me: ______________

☐ **Saturday** Date ______________ All I read today ______________

Best thing I marked today: *Reference* ______________

Thought: ______________

How it impressed me: ______________

MY READING HIGHLIGHTS

"Now, my children, listen to me. Those who follow my ways are happy. Listen to my teaching, and you will be wise. Do not ignore it. Those who listen to me are happy. They stand watching at my door every day. They are at my open door waiting to be with me." —Proverbs 8:32-34 (NCV)

Translation ______________________ Year __________

☐ **Sunday** Date ______________ All I read today ______________

Best thing I marked today: *Reference* ______________

Thought: ______________

____

How it impressed me: ______________

____

____

____

☐ **Monday** Date ______________ All I read today ______________

Best thing I marked today: *Reference* ______________

Thought: ______________

____

How it impressed me: ______________

____

____

____

____

☐ **Tuesday** Date ______________ All I read today ______________

Best thing I marked today: *Reference* ______________

Thought: ______________

____

How it impressed me: ______________

____

____

____

☐ **Wednesday** Date ______________ All I read today ______________

Best thing I marked today: *Reference* ______________

Thought: ______________

How it impressed me: ______________

☐ **Thursday** Date ______________ All I read today ______________

Best thing I marked today: *Reference* ______________

Thought: ______________

How it impressed me: ______________

☐ **Friday** Date ______________ All I read today ______________

Best thing I marked today: *Reference* ______________

Thought: ______________

How it impressed me: ______________

☐ **Saturday** Date ______________ All I read today ______________

Best thing I marked today: *Reference* ______________

Thought: ______________

How it impressed me: ______________

MY READING HIGHLIGHTS

"Now, my children, listen to me. Those who follow my ways are happy. Listen to my teaching, and you will be wise. Do not ignore it. Those who listen to me are happy. They stand watching at my door every day. They are at my open door waiting to be with me." —Proverbs 8:32-34 (NCV)

Translation ______________________________ Year __________

☐ **Sunday** Date ______________ All I read today ______________

Best thing I marked today: *Reference* ______________

Thought: ______________________________

____

How it impressed me: ______________________________

____

____

____

☐ **Monday** Date ______________ All I read today ______________

Best thing I marked today: *Reference* ______________

Thought: ______________________________

____

How it impressed me: ______________________________

____

____

____

____

☐ **Tuesday** Date ______________ All I read today ______________

Best thing I marked today: *Reference* ______________

Thought: ______________________________

____

How it impressed me: ______________________________

____

____

____

☐ **Wednesday** Date ______ All I read today ______

Best thing I marked today: *Reference* ______

Thought: ______

How it impressed me: ______

☐ **Thursday** Date ______ All I read today ______

Best thing I marked today: *Reference* ______

Thought: ______

How it impressed me: ______

☐ **Friday** Date ______ All I read today ______

Best thing I marked today: *Reference* ______

Thought: ______

How it impressed me: ______

☐ **Saturday** Date ______ All I read today ______

Best thing I marked today: *Reference* ______

Thought: ______

How it impressed me: ______

MY READING HIGHLIGHTS

"Now, my children, listen to me. Those who follow my ways are happy. Listen to my teaching, and you will be wise. Do not ignore it. Those who listen to me are happy. They stand watching at my door every day. They are at my open door waiting to be with me." —Proverbs 8:32-34 (NCV)

Translation ______ Year ______

☐ **Sunday** Date ______ All I read today ______

Best thing I marked today: *Reference* ______

Thought: ______

How it impressed me: ______

☐ **Monday** Date ______ All I read today ______

Best thing I marked today: *Reference* ______

Thought: ______

How it impressed me: ______

☐ **Tuesday** Date ______ All I read today ______

Best thing I marked today: *Reference* ______

Thought: ______

How it impressed me: ______

☐ **Wednesday** Date ______________ All I read today ______________

Best thing I marked today: *Reference* ______________

Thought: ______________

How it impressed me: ______________

☐ **Thursday** Date ______________ All I read today ______________

Best thing I marked today: *Reference* ______________

Thought: ______________

How it impressed me: ______________

☐ **Friday** Date ______________ All I read today ______________

Best thing I marked today: *Reference* ______________

Thought: ______________

How it impressed me: ______________

☐ **Saturday** Date ______________ All I read today ______________

Best thing I marked today: *Reference* ______________

Thought: ______________

How it impressed me: ______________

MY READING HIGHLIGHTS

"Now, my children, listen to me. Those who follow my ways are happy. Listen to my teaching, and you will be wise. Do not ignore it. Those who listen to me are happy. They stand watching at my door every day. They are at my open door waiting to be with me." —Proverbs 8:32-34 (NCV)

Translation ______________________ Year ________

☐ **Sunday** Date ______________ All I read today ______________

Best thing I marked today: *Reference* ______________

Thought: ______________

____

How it impressed me: ______________

____

____

____

☐ **Monday** Date ______________ All I read today ______________

Best thing I marked today: *Reference* ______________

Thought: ______________

____

How it impressed me: ______________

____

____

____

____

☐ **Tuesday** Date ______________ All I read today ______________

Best thing I marked today: *Reference* ______________

Thought: ______________

____

How it impressed me: ______________

____

____

____

☐ **Wednesday** Date ______ All I read today ______

Best thing I marked today: *Reference* ______

Thought: ______

How it impressed me: ______

☐ **Thursday** Date ______ All I read today ______

Best thing I marked today: *Reference* ______

Thought: ______

How it impressed me: ______

☐ **Friday** Date ______ All I read today ______

Best thing I marked today: *Reference* ______

Thought: ______

How it impressed me: ______

☐ **Saturday** Date ______ All I read today ______

Best thing I marked today: *Reference* ______

Thought: ______

How it impressed me: ______

MY READING HIGHLIGHTS

"Now, my children, listen to me. Those who follow my ways are happy. Listen to my teaching, and you will be wise. Do not ignore it. Those who listen to me are happy. They stand watching at my door every day. They are at my open door waiting to be with me." —Proverbs 8:32-34 (NCV)

Translation ______________________ Year ________

☐ **Sunday** Date ____________ All I read today ____________

Best thing I marked today: *Reference* ____________

Thought: ____________

How it impressed me: ____________

☐ **Monday** Date ____________ All I read today ____________

Best thing I marked today: *Reference* ____________

Thought: ____________

How it impressed me: ____________

☐ **Tuesday** Date ____________ All I read today ____________

Best thing I marked today: *Reference* ____________

Thought: ____________

How it impressed me: ____________

☐ **Wednesday** Date ______ All I read today ______

Best thing I marked today: *Reference* ______

Thought: ______

How it impressed me: ______

☐ **Thursday** Date ______ All I read today ______

Best thing I marked today: *Reference* ______

Thought: ______

How it impressed me: ______

☐ **Friday** Date ______ All I read today ______

Best thing I marked today: *Reference* ______

Thought: ______

How it impressed me: ______

☐ **Saturday** Date ______ All I read today ______

Best thing I marked today: *Reference* ______

Thought: ______

How it impressed me: ______

MY READING HIGHLIGHTS

"Now, my children, listen to me. Those who follow my ways are happy. Listen to my teaching, and you will be wise. Do not ignore it. Those who listen to me are happy. They stand watching at my door every day. They are at my open door waiting to be with me." —Proverbs 8:32-34 (NCV)

Translation ______________________ Year ________

☐ **Sunday** Date ____________ All I read today ____________

Best thing I marked today: *Reference* ____________

Thought: ____________

____

How it impressed me: ____________

____

____

____

☐ **Monday** Date ____________ All I read today ____________

Best thing I marked today: *Reference* ____________

Thought: ____________

____

How it impressed me: ____________

____

____

____

____

☐ **Tuesday** Date ____________ All I read today ____________

Best thing I marked today: *Reference* ____________

Thought: ____________

____

How it impressed me: ____________

____

____

____

☐ **Wednesday** Date ______ All I read today ______

Best thing I marked today: *Reference* ______

Thought: ______

How it impressed me: ______

☐ **Thursday** Date ______ All I read today ______

Best thing I marked today: *Reference* ______

Thought: ______

How it impressed me: ______

☐ **Friday** Date ______ All I read today ______

Best thing I marked today: *Reference* ______

Thought: ______

How it impressed me: ______

☐ **Saturday** Date ______ All I read today ______

Best thing I marked today: *Reference* ______

Thought: ______

How it impressed me: ______

MY READING HIGHLIGHTS

"Now, my children, listen to me. Those who follow my ways are happy. Listen to my teaching, and you will be wise. Do not ignore it. Those who listen to me are happy. They stand watching at my door every day. They are at my open door waiting to be with me." —Proverbs 8:32-34 (NCV)

Translation ________________________________ Year __________

☐ **Sunday** Date ______________ All I read today ______________

Best thing I marked today: *Reference* ______________

Thought: ______________________________

____

How it impressed me: ______________________________

____

____

____

☐ **Monday** Date ______________ All I read today ______________

Best thing I marked today: *Reference* ______________

Thought: ______________________________

____

How it impressed me: ______________________________

____

____

____

____

☐ **Tuesday** Date ______________ All I read today ______________

Best thing I marked today: *Reference* ______________

Thought: ______________________________

____

How it impressed me: ______________________________

____

____

____

☐ **Wednesday** Date ______ All I read today ______

Best thing I marked today: *Reference* ______

Thought: ______

How it impressed me: ______

☐ **Thursday** Date ______ All I read today ______

Best thing I marked today: *Reference* ______

Thought: ______

How it impressed me: ______

☐ **Friday** Date ______ All I read today ______

Best thing I marked today: *Reference* ______

Thought: ______

How it impressed me: ______

☐ **Saturday** Date ______ All I read today ______

Best thing I marked today: *Reference* ______

Thought: ______

How it impressed me: ______

MY READING HIGHLIGHTS

"Now, my children, listen to me. Those who follow my ways are happy. Listen to my teaching, and you will be wise. Do not ignore it. Those who listen to me are happy. They stand watching at my door every day. They are at my open door waiting to be with me." —Proverbs 8:32-34 (NCV)

Translation ________________________________ Year __________

☐ **Sunday** Date ______________ All I read today ______________

Best thing I marked today: *Reference* ______________

Thought: ________________________________

____

How it impressed me: ________________________________

____

____

____

☐ **Monday** Date ______________ All I read today ______________

Best thing I marked today: *Reference* ______________

Thought: ________________________________

____

How it impressed me: ________________________________

____

____

____

____

☐ **Tuesday** Date ______________ All I read today ______________

Best thing I marked today: *Reference* ______________

Thought: ________________________________

____

How it impressed me: ________________________________

____

____

____

☐ **Wednesday** Date ______________ All I read today ______________

Best thing I marked today: *Reference* ______________

Thought: ______________

How it impressed me: ______________

☐ **Thursday** Date ______________ All I read today ______________

Best thing I marked today: *Reference* ______________

Thought: ______________

How it impressed me: ______________

☐ **Friday** Date ______________ All I read today ______________

Best thing I marked today: *Reference* ______________

Thought: ______________

How it impressed me: ______________

☐ **Saturday** Date ______________ All I read today ______________

Best thing I marked today: *Reference* ______________

Thought: ______________

How it impressed me: ______________

MY READING HIGHLIGHTS

"Now, my children, listen to me. Those who follow my ways are happy. Listen to my teaching, and you will be wise. Do not ignore it. Those who listen to me are happy. They stand watching at my door every day. They are at my open door waiting to be with me." —Proverbs 8:32-34 (NCV)

Translation ______________________ Year ________

☐ **Sunday** Date ______________ All I read today ______________

Best thing I marked today: *Reference* ______________

Thought: ______________

How it impressed me: ______________

☐ **Monday** Date ______________ All I read today ______________

Best thing I marked today: *Reference* ______________

Thought: ______________

How it impressed me: ______________

☐ **Tuesday** Date ______________ All I read today ______________

Best thing I marked today: *Reference* ______________

Thought: ______________

How it impressed me: ______________

☐ **Wednesday** Date ______ All I read today ______

Best thing I marked today: *Reference* ______

Thought: ______

How it impressed me: ______

☐ **Thursday** Date ______ All I read today ______

Best thing I marked today: *Reference* ______

Thought: ______

How it impressed me: ______

☐ **Friday** Date ______ All I read today ______

Best thing I marked today: *Reference* ______

Thought: ______

How it impressed me: ______

☐ **Saturday** Date ______ All I read today ______

Best thing I marked today: *Reference* ______

Thought: ______

How it impressed me: ______

MY READING HIGHLIGHTS

"Now, my children, listen to me. Those who follow my ways are happy. Listen to my teaching, and you will be wise. Do not ignore it. Those who listen to me are happy. They stand watching at my door every day. They are at my open door waiting to be with me." —Proverbs 8:32-34 (NCV)

Translation ______________________ Year ________

☐ **Sunday** Date ______________ All I read today ______________

Best thing I marked today: *Reference* ______________

Thought: ______________

____

How it impressed me: ______________

____

____

____

☐ **Monday** Date ______________ All I read today ______________

Best thing I marked today: *Reference* ______________

Thought: ______________

____

How it impressed me: ______________

____

____

____

____

☐ **Tuesday** Date ______________ All I read today ______________

Best thing I marked today: *Reference* ______________

Thought: ______________

____

How it impressed me: ______________

____

____

____

☐ **Wednesday** Date ______________ All I read today ______________

Best thing I marked today: *Reference* ______________

Thought: ______________

How it impressed me: ______________

☐ **Thursday** Date ______________ All I read today ______________

Best thing I marked today: *Reference* ______________

Thought: ______________

How it impressed me: ______________

☐ **Friday** Date ______________ All I read today ______________

Best thing I marked today: *Reference* ______________

Thought: ______________

How it impressed me: ______________

☐ **Saturday** Date ______________ All I read today ______________

Best thing I marked today: *Reference* ______________

Thought: ______________

How it impressed me: ______________

PRAYER SHEET

REQUEST	GOD'S ANSWER

PRAYER SHEET

REQUEST	GOD'S ANSWER

PRAYER SHEET

REQUEST	GOD'S ANSWER

PRAYER SHEET

REQUEST	GOD'S ANSWER

PRAYER SHEET

REQUEST	GOD'S ANSWER

PRAYER SHEET

REQUEST	GOD'S ANSWER

NOTES

1. *Webster's New World Dictionary*, 2nd college edition, s.v. "integrity."

NCM
NAVIGATOR **CHURCH** MINISTRIES

NCM focuses on helping churches become more intentional in discipleship and outreach. NCM staff help pastors, church leaders, and lifelong laborers across the United States develop an effective and personalized approach to accomplishing the Great Commission.

NCM works alongside the local church to grow intentional disciplemaking cultures, as reflected in the following illustration:

Growing *intentional* Disciplemaking Cultures

A process to help churches send laborers into their communities

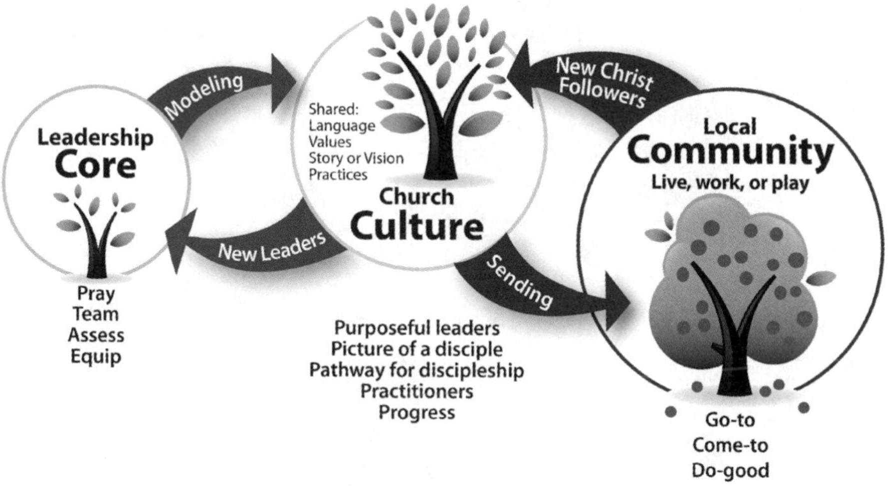

NCM also offers seminars, materials, and coaching to help the local church see discipleship flourish in successive generations. See our web page for further information on how NCM can help you.

www.navigators.org/ncm
or e-mail to ncm@navigators.org
or call our NCM Office at (719) 594-2446
or write to PO Box 6000, Colorado Springs, CO 80934

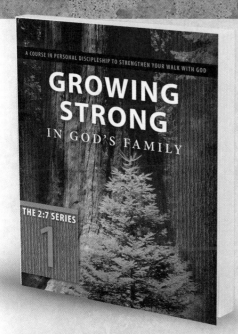

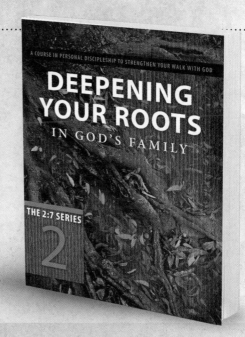